James Archibald Sidey

Mistura Curiosa

Being a Higgledy-Piggledy of Scotch, Irish, English, Nigger ...

James Archibald Sidey

Mistura Curiosa

Being a Higgledy-Piggledy of Scotch, Irish, English, Nigger ...

ISBN/EAN: 9783744728997

Printed in Europe, USA, Canada, Australia, Japan

Cover: Foto ©ninafisch / pixelio.de

More available books at **www.hansebooks.com**

MISTURA·CURIOSA

EDINBURGH:
MACLACHLAN AND STEWART, SOUTH BRIDGE.

TYPO. . . CRAWFORD AND M'CABE, GEORGE STREET.
LITHO. . . G. WATERSTON AND SON, HANOVER STREET.

ENTERED AT STATIONERS' HALL.

MISTURA CURIOSA

BEING A

HIGGLEDY PIGGLEDY

OF

SCOTTISH ENGLISH NIGGER GOLFING SCHURCOMIC

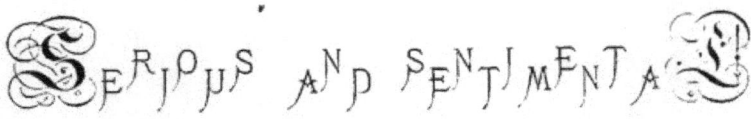

SERIOUS AND SENTIMENTAL

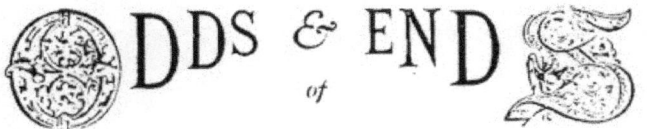

ODDS & ENDS

of

RHYMES AND FABLES

BY F. CRUCELLI,

WITH ILLUSTRATIONS BY

CHARLES ALTAMONT DOYLE AND JOHN

EDINBURGH:
MACLACHLAN AND STEWART.
1869.

Preface and Dedication.

SENSIBLE Subscriber and Intelligent Purchaser, it would ill become me to begrudge you a little grumble, if (*after* having paid your money) you are not content, either with the quality or the quantity of the odds and ends which enter into the composition of this book; but you will please to remember that they were written, not for your benefit, but for my amusement, as sometime ago I *did* find out that there was a deal of truth in the old saying,

"*All work and no play makes Jack a dull boy.*"

Not that it has made very much difference on me, so far as I can discover, but it has made me sharp enough to prefer two requests,—1st, that should you be inclined to give any praise, all and every portion thereof should be bestowed on *me* for my share of the work: 2d, that should you be inclined to give any blame, all and every portion thereof should be thrown on to the shoulders of CHARLES DOYLE and JOHN SMART, who, by their Sketches have induced me to publish. I freely admit that some of the verses may be thin or poor, but that is counterbalanced by the large amount of dissipation in others; be that as it may, whether you approve or not, I bear you no ill will, as a proof thereof I request you will allow me to dedicate this

𝔅umper to your very good 𝔥ealth.

𝔍. 𝔈.

Contents

	Illustrated by	Page
Bluebeard,	C. A. Doyle,	1
The Irish Schoolmaster,	C. A. Doyle,	6
The Little Beggar Girl,	J. Smart,	10
The Bears and the Bees,	C. A. Doyle,	12
Shades,	C. A. Doyle,	17
Tom Thumb,	C. A. Doyle,	19
Mabel,	J. Smart,	22
Ye Entreaty,	C. A. Doyle,	23
Mick Maloony,	C. A. Doyle,	25
Welcome is Winter,	J. Smart,	28
Rest, Baby Rest,	C. A. Doyle,	30
D'ye Twig,	C. A. Doyle,	32
The Drooping Flower,	J. Smart.	35
Come Watch the Moonbeams,	C. A. Doyle,	36
Sweet Nell,	C. A. Doyle,	38
Ye Wolf and ye Child,	C. A. Doyle,	40
Hame's Aye Hame,	J. Smart,	42
Lubly Topsy,	C. A. Doyle,	44
The Whale,	C. A. Doyle,	47
Tilly Fell,	J. Smart,	50
A Golden Rule in Golf,	C. A. Doyle,	52
The Snow Flake,	C. A. Doyle,	55
The Bonnie Bairnie,	C. A. Doyle,	56
Scotland's Bonnie Broom,	J. Smart,	58
The Brewing o' the "Tun,"	C. A. Doyle,	60

	Illustrated by	Page
The Ruin of the "Tum,"	C. A. Doyle,	63
Ye Fox and ye Grapes,	C. A. Doyle,	64
The Music o' the Curling Tee,	J. Smart,	68
Do Angels bid them come?	J. Smart,	69
Wee Nannie,	C. A. Doyle,	70
The Wayward Boy,	C. A. Doyle,	73
Auld Scotch Tunes,	C. A. Doyle,	75
Oh Tempora! Oh Mores,	C. A. Doyle,	76
Oh! hey for a crack with a Lass,	C. A. Doyle,	80
The Dewdrop,	J. Smart,	83
Old Friends and Tried Friends,	C. A. Doyle,	84
The return Home of the Wanderer,	C. A. Doyle,	86
The T, Teetotaleer,	C. A. Doyle,	88
The Gude Gaun Game o' Curling,	C. A. Doyle,	90
Dinah Vhoe,	J. Smart,	92
My Ain Wee Bairn,	C. A. Doyle,	94
The Long Putt Sly,	C. A. Doyle,	96
The Grinderpest,	C. A. Doyle,	99
The Auld Fail Dyke,	J. Smart,	102
A Highland Mother's Lament,	J. Smart,	104
Ye Sheep and ye Crow,	C. A. Doyle,	106
A Gude Game Yet,	C. A. Doyle,	108
The Herring Fisher,	C. A. Doyle,	110
East and West,	C. A. Doyle,	112
The Last Farewell,	J. Smart,	115
Johnny Graham,	C. A. Doyle,	116
Bygones,	C. A. Doyle,	118
The Yachtsman,	C. A. Doyle,	120
Ye Hare and ye Tortoise,	C. A. Doyle,	122
Oh! How I've Longed for Thee,	C. A. Doyle,	125
The Standard of Britain,	C. A. Doyle,	126
Nelly Leigh,	J. Smart,	128
The Hills of Dee,	C. A. Doyle,	130
De Han'some Niggers,	C. A. Doyle,	132
My First Match,	C. A. Doyle,	134
Jeddart Jock,	J. Smart,	136
Whisky Oh!	C. A. Doyle,	138
The MicMacIntosh, ch,	C. A. Doyle,	140
Jock Tamson,	C. A. Doyle,	143

	Illustrated by	Page
The Museum, . .	C. A. DOYLE,	. 146
Life, . . .	J. SMART,	. 151
The Jolly Lot, ...	C. A. DOYLE,	. 152
The Great may hae their Palaces,	C. A. DOYLE,	. 154
The Curler's Grip, . .	C. A. DOYLE,	. 156
Our Hielandmen, . . .	C. A. DOYLE,	. 158
I'm Weary, Weary Waiting, .	J. SMART,	. 160
Ye Fox and ye Crow, . . .	C. A. DOYLE,	. 162
The Angel says "Come," .	C. A. DOYLE,	. 165
Our Auld Punch Bowl, . .	C. A. DOYLE,	. 166
When Summer Suns are Dying, .	C. A. DOYLE,	. 168
Goodnight, . . .	C. A. DOYLE,	. 170

The Frontispiece, the illustrations of the Preface, and following pages, viz.,—20, 24, 60, 63, 82, 84, 85, 91, 101, 106, 107, 110, 111, 136, 143, 145, 147, 148, 149, 150, 151, 155, 159, 168, and 170, are Photo-lithographs.

Yᵉ only authentic account of yᵉ Life and Adventures of
"BLUEBEARD,"
Or, as yᵉ Story Book says, " yᵉ effects of Female Curiosity."

AIR 1.—*"In a cottage near a wood."*

Slick in the middle of a jolly big wood,
   There Mr Bluebeard's castle stood.
The walls were of brick, the doors were of wood,
The windows of plate glass, strong and good:
And slick in the middle of a jolly big wood,
   There Mr Bluebeard's castle stood.

AIR 2.—*" The days we went a gipseying "*

And the house itself was furnish-ed
   So very trim and neat,
You'd almost thought he'd ordered it,
   From Scott's in George's Street;
But then you see that couldn't be,
   For Scott he didn't know,
In the days he went a furnishing,
   A long time ago.
     In the days he went a furnishing,
       A long time ago.

AIR 3.—"*The old English Gentleman.*"

And there Bluebeard, he reigned supreme
  O'er house, and hall, and stable;
And every night his custom was
  To lie below the table.
Until at last his servants came
  And carried him off to bed.
When he awoke next morning with
  Such a pa-in in his head—
Like a true blue blazing Bluebeard.
  A cove of the true blue breed.

AIR 4.- "*There's nae luck about the house.*"

At length old Blue said to himself
  "I'll go and take a wife,"
"Altho' that I know very well"
  "She'll plague me all my life."
So off he set and got Miss Moll,
  Though rather short and weighty,
A tender, squinting, one-eyed maid
  About the age of eighty.

But very shortly after that
  Says he " O here's a go,"
" The married life it don't suit me,"
  " It is so precious slow,"
"So I'll go off with Billy Jones"
  "And have a jolly spree, "
"And its likely that I won't be back "
  " For a day, or two, or three."

AIR 5.—"*Oh what a row, what a rumpus,*" etc.

"But what a row, what a rumpus, and a rioting"
"I will kick up, you may be sure, when I come back."
"But what a row, what a rumpus, and a rioting"
"I will kick up, you may be sure, when I come back."

"If I hear you've been and asked those Browns and Greens to tea with you,"
"I'll tell you what, I won't stand that, so now beware of what you do;"
"For should you come all for to go and look into that press, ma'am,"
"You'll get yourself, as Pompey said, into a pretty mess, ma'am."
Chorus. "And such a row, such a rumpus, and a rioting"
"I will kick up, you may be sure, when I come back."

AIR 6.—"*Lord Lovel.*"

But he'd scarcely been gone when she open'd the press,
    And straightway fell into a "swound,"
When she saw all Bluebeard's wives, like coats
    On pegs, all hanging around, round, round, etc.

AIR 7.—"*Nid noddin.*"

And they're a' hanging, hang, hang, hanging,
    And they're a' hanging up against the wall,
And they're a' hanging, hang, hang, hanging,
    And they're a' hanging up against the wall.
Now some were in quarters, and some were in halves,
There were four and twenty heads, and eight and forty calves.
Chorus. And they're a' hanging, hang, hang, hanging,
    And they're a' hanging up against the wall.

AIR 8.—*"Sprig of Sheldah."*

But it happened next day, when old Bluebeard came back,
That he found Mrs Bluebeard with a brick-bat
    A scrubbing away at a bloody old key,
    A scrubbing away at a bloody old key.
"Goodness gracious," she cried, "pray don't murder me,"
"And oh, sweetest William, I pray your mercy,"
"The key went itself and it opened the door,"
"And I only looked in, and I've done nothing more"
    "But scrub all this day at this bloody old key,"
    "But scrub all this day at this bloody old key."

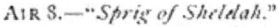

Old Bluebeard was savage and wroth as a Turk,
And he swore by his beard, that his wife he would Burke;
    His nice little wife only eighty years old,
    His nice little wife only eighty years old.
But two brothers of hers, who had just come to dine,
Rushed up the stairs, crying, "oh Lord, here's a shine,"
So out went their swords and off went his head,
And as a matter in course old Bluebeard was dead.
    And his wife left a widow, just eighty years old,
    And his wife left a widow, just eighty years old.

AIR 9.—"*Lord Lovel.*"

And now that old Bluebeard is gone and is dead—
    I'll tell you the cause of his death;
Some say that he died for want of his head,
    And some say for want of his breath, 'reath, 'reath,
        And some say for want of his breath.

This tale may be true, or this tale may be false,
    Or this tale may be all a lie;
But one of the worst faults a woman can have
    Is cu-ri-os-i-ty-ty-y,
        Is cu-ri-os-i-ty.

THE IRISH SCHOOLMASTER.

AIR—"*The Young May Moon.*"

Come here, my boy, hould up your head,
   And look like a jintleman, Sir,
Just tell me who "King David" was,
   Now tell me if you can, Sir?
King David was a mighty man,
   And he was King of Spain, Sir,
His eldest daughter, "Jessie" was
   The "flower of Dunblane," Sir.

You're right, my boy, hould up your head,
   And look like a jintleman, Sir,
"Sir Isaac Newton," who was he,
   Now tell me if you can, Sir?
Sir Isaac Newton was the boy,
   That climbed the apple tree, Sir,
He then fell down, and broke his crown,
   And lost his gravity, Sir.

You're right, my boy, hould up your head,
   And look like a jintleman, Sir,
Just tell me who old "Marmion" was,
   Now tell me if you can, Sir?
Old Marmion was a soldier bold,
   But he went all to pot, Sir,
He was hanged upon the gallows tree,
   For killing Sir Walter Scott, Sir.

You're right, my boy, hould up your head,
    And look like a jintleman, Sir,
Just tell me who "Sir Rob Roy" was,
    Now tell me, if you can, Sir?
Sir Rob Roy was a tailor to
    The King of the Cannibal Islands,
He spoiled a pair of breeches, and
    Was banished to the Highlands.

You're right, my boy, hould up your head,
    And look like a jintleman, Sir,
Then "Bonaparte," who was he,
    Now tell me if you can, Sir?
Old Bonaparte was King of France,
    Before the Revolution,
But he was kilt at Waterloo,
    Which ruined his constitution.

You're right, my boy, hould up your head,
    And look like a jintleman, Sir,
Just tell me who "King Jonah" was,
    Now tell me if you can, Sir?
King Jonah was the strongest man,
    That ever wore a crown, Sir,
For though the whale did swallow him,
    It couldn't keep him down, Sir.

You're right, my boy, hould up your head,
   And look like a jintleman, Sir,
Just tell me who that "Moses" was,
   Now tell me if you can, Sir?
Sure Moses was the Christian name
   Of good King Pharaoh's daughter,
She was a milkmaid, and she took
   A profit from the water.

You're right, my boy, hould up your head,
   And look like a jintleman, Sir,
Just tell me now where "Dublin" is,
   Now tell me if you can, Sir?
Och! Dublin is a town in Cork,
   And built upon the Equator,
It's close to mount Vesuvius,
   And watered by the "Cratur."

You're right, my boy, hould up your head,
   And look like a jintleman, Sir,
Just tell me now where "London" is,
   Now tell me if you can, Sir?
Och! London is a town in Spain,
   'Twas lost in the earthquake, Sir,
The Cockneys murther the English there,
   Whenever they do spake, Sir.

You're right, my boy, hould up your head,
    You're now a jintleman, Sir,
For in history and geography,
    I've taught you all I can, Sir.
And if any one should ask you now,
    Where you got all your knowledge,
Just tell them 'twas from " Paddy Blake,"
    Of " Bally Blarney College."

May be sung to the tune of " Kitty Mooney."

THE LITTLE BEGGAR GIRL.

An incident during last year's frost.

SHALL I tell a tale that seems to vie
  With the widow's mite of old—
A tale of truth, that met my eye
  One wintry night so cold,
    When the frost and sleet,
    Chill'd the wandering feet,
      Of the little beggar girl?

CHILL'D the wandering feet of the beggar girl,,
  And the hearts of the passers by,
Though they saw grief lurking 'neath each curl,
  And hunger in her eye,
    So mutely crave
    One penny to save
      The little beggar girl.

ONE penny to save! but all passed by,
  Till a strong, big-hearted man,
Saw the dying gleam in her sunken eye,
  And stopt his lumbering van;
    Then the first kind word
    In her life she heard
      Touched the heart of the beggar girl.

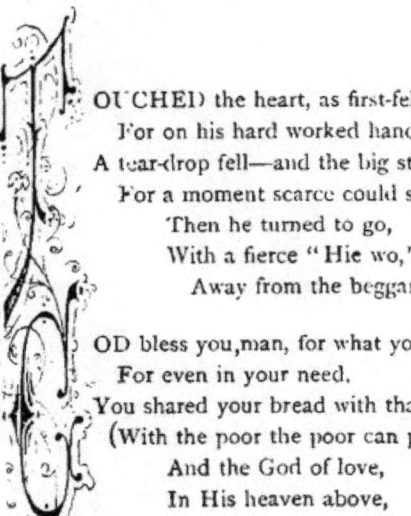

TOUCHED the heart, as first-felt kindness can,
   For on his hard worked hand
A tear-drop fell—and the big strong man,
   For a moment scarce could stand;
      Then he turned to go,
      With a fierce "Hie wo,"
         Away from the beggar girl.

GOD bless you, man, for what you've done,
   For even in your need,
You shared your bread with that orphan one,
   (With the poor the poor can plead.)
      And the God of love,
      In His heaven above,
      Marked your act of love
         To the little beggar girl.

Edinr. 1862.

THE BEARS AND THE BEES.

ANE FABLE.

THERE lived two bears a long time back,
    The vildest boys in all the town;
The name of von vas Billy Black,
    The tother's name vas Tommy Brown.

Now them two boys vas no relation,
    Although they looked like brothers two,
And each von in his sitivation
    Played all the mischief he could do.

Vell—vone day they vent a valking,
    The lovely fields all for to see,
And jist as they vas busy talking,
    Young Tommy Brown he caught a bee.

Vith vonder seen in every feature,
    "Crikey, Bill," young Tommy said,
"It surely is some vondrous creature,
    P'raps it is a quadruped."

"Oh, oh!" said Villiam, "you're another;
　Vy, it is a honey bee;
Don't you remember that your mother
　Taught this little hymn to thee :

"How much the little busy beeses
　Do improve each shining hour,
And gather honey 'mong the treeses,
　All day from the opening flower."

"Vell," said Bill, "ve aint no money,
　And can't get nothing for to eat,
Let's go and try and find some honey-
　Comb, for it is wery sweet."

Avay they vent o'er fields and ditches,
　Over hedges and sich like,
Bill lost his cap, Tom tore his breeches,
　Ven they found a bumbee's byke.

They pulled and tore it all to pieces,
    Till they found the honey-comb,
Ven fathers, mothers, sisters, nieces,
    All rushed out to fight for home.

Now Villiam heard the beeses humming,
    And quickly hid himself from view,
But Tom he didn't see them coming,
    So on poor Tom each varrior flew.

He filled the vood vith yells and screeches,
    For they stung his arms and thighs,
Down his back and up his breeches,
    And quickly closed up both his eyes.

Now ven Tom vas busy crying,
    And vith rage and pain did foam,
Villiam he vas busy trying,
    All for to get the honey-comb.

At length he got it all secure.
  Ven Tom's figure met his sight,
Says he, "I vish them bees vas fewer,
  For you're in an awful plight.

"But run and lie down in the river.
  It hardly reaches to your knees;
It's the only way that you can ever
  Rid yourself of all them bees."

So Tom he quickly disappeared,
  As in the river he lay flat,
Except his nose vich jist appeared;
  It vould not do to submerge that.

The beeses then vere quite astounded
  To see him wanish out of sight,
And as each thought that Tom was drownded,
  Each von said, "It sarved him right."

Ven they vas gone Bill 'gan a hauling
   Half-drowned Thomas to the shore,
So home together they vent crawling,
   And vowing ne'er to vander more.

Yet poor Thomas loved some funning,
   For ven Bill said, "He'd go snacks,"
Tom he replied, "Excuse my punning,"
   "You've got the honey, I the whacks."

Some folks may think this 'ere's a crammer,
   And vont svallow any down,
But jist ask Tom, he's sure to stammer,
   "It's true, as my name's
                    B—B—Brown."

Shades.

There is a shade on a brow once bright,
  On a mother's brow this day;
But 'tis only seen in the broad clear light,
  And not in that chamber grey.
    In that chamber grey,
    Where her loved one lay,
      Wearing away.

There is a shade on that bad man's brow,
  A deep, dark shade and a gloom;
And he'd give the world to raise it now,
  And bury it in the tomb.
    For, dark as the tomb
    Is that lonely room
      Where lies his doom.

There was a shade on that gentle brow,
  It has passed, to return no more;
For the heavenly gleams are shining now,
  That lightened the burden sore.
    And the burden sore,
    Which on earth she bore,
      She feels no more.

There is a shade 'neath the aged yew,
　　That stands near the church alone,
And it falls on the weeds, and rank grass, too,
　　Where lies a moss-covered stone;
　　　　And there, now unknown,
　　　　Sleeps one alone—

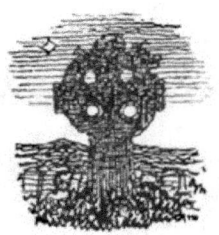

"Beneath this stone."

Yᵉ LIFE AND ADVENTURES
OF
TOM THUMB.

AIR—"*Laird o' Cockpen.*"

There once lived a man, and he was a small 'un,
And some folks would say he was'nt a tall (at all) 'un;
But his life and his deeds were so very "rum,"
He was "50 O. P.," this little Tom Thumb.

'Tis said that he lived on bacon and beans;
And sometimes he dined on salt pork and greens,
But he thought that such feeding was rather humdrum,
"I've gone the whole hog," said little Tom Thumb.

The story books tell how the brindled cow ate him,
But that is all wrong, for a sheep first did get him;
Which is proved by his words, though 'tis doubted by some,
"I've walked into his mutton," said little Tom Thumb.

One day, as his mother was making some paste,
Tom fell into it, as he wanted to taste,
So he was mixed up, as he looked like a crumb,
"I'm off on the batter," said little Tom Thumb.

His mother then covered a pie with the crust,
Put it into the oven, when out her son burst,
He looked rather warm, but he cried out "By gum,"
"Done brown, I declare," said little Tom Thumb.

A pedlar came past, said the "pie is bewitched,"
Put it into his bag, then suddenly hitched
It over his shoulder, walked off with his chum,
"It's over the left," said little Tom Thumb.

As Tom once was crossing a river close by,
A salmon snapt at him, as it would a fly;
But as it was dark, Tom sang rather mum,
"I'm down in the mouth," said little Tom Thumb.

Next day a black raven poor Tom did espy,
Which carried him up in the heaven so high;
If the bird let him go, to the ground he would come,
"I'll be dashed if I do," said little Tom Thumb.

But just at the time when the bird let him go,
A cook, with a basin of broth, passed below,
Tom fell into it, straight down as a plumb,
"I'm a broth of a boy," said little Tom Thumb.

The cook got a fright, and he lost all his wits;
At least, what he had were all smashed to bits;
For he thought, in his face he'd got all the scum,
"It's all in my eye," said little Tom Thumb.

He grabbed at poor Tom, and took him to town,
And swore in a waterbutt he would him drown;
But water was scarce, not enough for a "Tum,"
"It's all up the spout," said little Tom Thumb.

But at last a whole regiment of soldiers came round,
And from that day to this Tom's never been found;
But I've heard said, that he lives in the drum,
"I'm bound up in parchment," said little Tom Thumb.

This tale may be long for such a short man,
And yet I've curtailed it as much as I can;
But of poor little Tom, you've the whole total sum;
So that's the sum total of little Tom Thumb.

"MABEL."

WHEN first I saw my Mabel fair,
    Oh! the blossoms bloomed bright on the hawthorn tree,
The lark sang sweet in the sunny air,
    And the waves danced light o'er the rippling sea.
        Oh! gentle Mabel kind and true,
        With trusting eyes of heavenly blue,
        Tho' long I stray in lands afar,
        Thou'lt be for aye my guiding star.

When last I saw my Mabel kind,
    Oh! the blossoms were decayed on the hawthorn tree,
The lark was mute in the wintry wind,
    And the billows raged wild o'er the stormy sea.
        Oh! gentle Mabel kind and true,
        With trusting eyes of heavenly blue,
        Tho' long I stray in lands afar,
        Thou'lt be for aye my guiding star.

Then fare-thee-well, my Mabel true,
    When the blossoms bloom again on the hawthorn tree,
When the lark from its wings shakes the summer's dew,
    I'll come back again o'er the dark blue sea.
        Oh! gentle Mabel kind and true,
        With trusting eyes of heavenly blue,
        Tho' long I stray in lands afar,
        Thou'lt be for aye my guiding star.

Yᵉ ENTREATY.

Cast me not from thee now,
    Bid me not go,
Spare, spare my breaking heart
    This pang of woe;
Think of those happy times.
    When all alone,
Words that were loving said.
    Thou we'rt my own.

Cast me not from thee now,
    Bid me but stay,
What is this world when thou
    Art far away;
Death would be better than
    Life without thee,
Life has no joys when thou
    Art lost to me.

Cast me not from thee now,
    Let us not part,
Take me once more again,
    Back to thy heart;
Let me but feel that I'm
    Still dear to thee,
What is this life when thou,
    Lost art to me.

EXTRA VERSE.

Oh! spare my breaking heart, crush me no more,
    Bruised as my spirit's been, sadly and sore;
Still have I ever proved faithful and true,—
    Kiss me, and order then, supper for two.

MICK MALOONY.

AIR—"*Rory o' More.*"

Och! sure and I am in a terrible state
   With picking and choosing 'twixt Kitty and Kate,
For in troth I am tould, both cannot be had,
   I must only take one—och! an' sure an' bedad
If I had but known, that that was their plan,
   I'd never been born an Irishman,
I'd rather been Russian, Turk, or a Jew,
   T'would have saved me some bother, to have taken the two.
      But I'm ready ye'll find, if yees have a mind,
         Jist to tread on the tail of my coat this same night;
      For och! an' its true, what I'm telling to you,
         So lay hoult of me, boys, for I'm going to fight.

There's Kitty is fair, and Kate she is dark,
   And Kitty is quiet, Kate fond of a lark,
But when each of them foot it so light and so smart,
   Faith they both take another step into my heart.
For each are quite perfect in eyes and in lip,
   And each have their noses, "*snub*lime" at the tip,
If you saw but the tother, you'd sware 'twas the one,
   Och! thunder and turf now, what's to be done!
        But I'm ready ye'll find, if yees have a mind,
           Jist to tread on the tail of my coat this same night;
        For och! an' its true, what I'm telling to you,
           So lay hoult of me, boys, for I'm going to fight.

Says I to myself, sure I'm at a loss,
   Jist lend me a penny, and I'll have a toss,
Here's heads for the dark, and there's tails for the fair,
   Och! the devil a head or a tail is there there.
But I must look sharp, and be up to the scratch,
   Else my pipe will be out for want of a match;
Faith I'll just cut this minute, for if I don't mind,
   They'll be both off before me, while I'm left behind.
        But I'm ready ye'll find, if yees have a mind,
           Jist to tread on the tail of my coat this same night;
        For och! an' its true, what I'm telling to you,
           So lay hoult of me, boys, for I'm going to fight.

'Then sure an' I'll be in a terrible state,
  If with picking and choosing I'm rather too late,
An' in troth as I find, both cannot be had,
  I'll only take one—and that same isn't bad.
An', och! by the piper, 'twill be a foine sight,
  To hear Mick Maloony's wild scraim of delight,
When he gets himself married, in church to a bride,
  And finds, 'tis a rib that's a-tickling his side.
        But I'm ready ye'll find, if yees have a mind,
            Jist to tread on the tail of my coat this same night;
          For och! an' its true, what I'm telling to you,
            So lay hoult of me, boys, for I'm going to fight.

WELCOME IS WINTER.

Air—*Hail to the Chief.*

WELCOME is Winter, when Autumn's decaying
   Lays bare ilka tree to the black frosts o' nicht.
Welcome is winter, when cauld blasts are swaying
   The lang leafless branches, aneth the moon licht,
        For syne comes auld Johnnie,
        Sae kindly and bonnie,
And haps them a' up in his plaiden o' snaw.
        For warm is his rachen,
        On hill, glen and clachan,
Oh Winter is welcome, to curlers an' a'.

Welcome is winter, for wee flowers are sleeping,
   Sae cosie and warm aneth auld Johnnie's wing;
Till waked by the sound of the icicles weeping,
   Their een' open wide, at the first blink o' spring.
        Then ilka bird singing,
        The echoes saft ringing,
Gie thanks to the kind hearts, for crumbs as they fa'.
        In words never weary,
        But blythesome and cheerie,
Oh Winter is welcome, to curlers an' a'.

Come Curlers, come then, baith married and single,
    And welcome auld Johnnie, wi' hearty gude cheer;
For soon we'll delight in the bricht blazing ingle,
    And cosie fireside, now that winter is near.
        Then up in the morning
        Baith care and toil scornin'
We'll meet wi' our brithers frae cot and frae ha';
        For warm hearts are beating,
        To bid us kind greeting,
Oh Winter is welcome, to curlers an' a'.

"REST, BABY REST."

AIR—"*Aye Wakin' O.*"

REST, baby rest.
   God His watch is keeping
     O'er thee day and night;
   O'er thee wake or sleeping,
         Rest, baby rest.
   As the hours glide on,
   Softly o'er thee creeping;
   May'st thou love to learn
To trust His watchful keeping.
         Rest, baby rest.

REST, baby rest.
   God His watch is keeping
     O'er thee day and night;
   O'er thee wake or sleeping,
          Rest, baby rest.
   And as years fleet past,
   Swift beyond recalling,
   May'st thou in Him trust,
Thy feet to keep from falling.
          Rest, baby rest.

REST, baby rest.
   God His watch is keeping
     O'er thee day and night;
   O'er thee wake or sleeping,
          Rest, baby rest.
   When thy sands have run,
   Round thee friends still weeping,
   May'st thou sleep for aye
In His eternal keeping.
          Rest, baby rest.

"D'YE TWIG?"

Air—"*The days we went a gipseying.*"

Oh I'm a little simple girl from the country just come down,
And am not up to dodges like most servant maids in town.
My Missus said, "no followers," but I did'nt care one fig,
For one can scarce exist without "one's cousins,"—hem !—D'ye twig?
For one can scarce exist without "one's cousins,"—Don't ye twig?

Well, next day as my missus chanced, to come home rather late,
She caught my "cousin Sam" and me a-standing at the gate.
Poor Sam, he very quickly cut, but I didn't care one fig,
For "sister Jane" had come that night to see me,—hem !—D'ye twig?
For "sister Jane" had come that night to see me,—Don't ye twig?

So missus to the kitchen came,—what missuses should not do;
And found that "sister Jane" then wore top boots and whiskers too.
Of course I really felt much shocked, but I didn't care one fig.
For Watchman number 84 was waiting,—hem!—D'ye twig?
For Watchman number 84 was waiting,—Don't ye twig?

Misfortunes never singly come, for soon an awful sneeze
Came from the watchman in the press half choked with bread and cheese.
My missus soon discovered him, but I didn't care one fig,
For what's life worth to girls, unless they've "cousins"—hem Dy'e twig?
For what's life worth to girls, unless they've "cousins"—Don't ye twig?

My missus gave me warning then "no followin-ging," said she;
But 'twasn't me as followed them, 'twas them as followed me.
And so next week I leave this place, but I do not care one fig,
For Sam, he says, his house just wants a missus,—hem!—D'ye twig?
For Sam, he says, his house just wants a missus,—Don't ye twig?

"The Drooping Flower."

POOR drooping bud, and art thou doomed
   So soon to wither and decay,
Whil'st thy companions fair have bloomed,
   In strength and beauty day by day,
Alas! that one so young should fade,
   Ere yet thy life had scarce begun;
But cruel hands on thee were laid,
   And bruised thee sore, my only one.

I'll raise thee now with gentle care,
   And lean thee on thy parent stem,
Perchance the balmy summer air
   May waft thee health, my little gem.
Ah yes! if friendly love and care,
   Were oftener shown to frail and weak,
The broken heart less oft would share,
   Its sickened griefs, with hectic cheek.

COME, WATCH THE MOONBEAMS PLAYING.

COME, come, come!
  Come watch the moonbeams playing,
O'er hill and valley straying
    While all is still—
While all is still,
  And not a sound
On heath and hill
  Is heard around—
    Is heard around.

    Come, come, come,
While not a sound is heard around
  In glade or wooded dale;
For silence breathes its stillness o'er
  Each flowery mead and vale.
And everything in Nature seems
Asleep, except the merry moonbeams;
And everything in nature seems
Asleep, except the merry moonbeams.
  For winds are hushed, and songsters sweet
    At eve have gone to rest,
  With tiny head, 'neath folded wing
    On downy pillow pressed—
      On downy pillow pressed.

COME, come, come,
Come watch the moonbeams playing,
Over the bright sea straying;
  While every wave
    With rippling lips
  Kisses the beam
    That lightly trips
  Over the moonlit sea
  In laughing mirth and glee.
And the sands on the shore afar are seen
Like a bright, bright cord of silver sheen;
  While every wave with rippling lips
  Kisses the beam that lightly trips
    Over the moonlit sea.

    Then come, come, come,
Come watch the moonbeams playing,
O'er hill and valley straying.
Playing, straying, never staying,
  Wandering lightly on with glee;
Playing, straying—never staying,
  Wandering over land and sea.
    Then come, come, come!

SWEET NELL OR THE GROCER'S DAUGHTER.

A DUET.

Joe loq

AIR—"*Sensation Duet.*"

OH I shall turn quite crazy,
   Insane, stark staring mad,
For Nell, the duck-y-daisy
   Has treated me so bad;
For guess the answer that she gave
   When I popped the question sweet,
"This is a very fine day Joe,
   But *how are your poor feet.*"

Jim loq.—

Never say die, never say die, but keep your mind serene Joe,
Though strange it is, a swell like you, should be so jolly green Joe
Never say die, never say die, for Nell, the grocer's daughter;
There's just as good fish in the sea, as ever came out of the water.

Joe

BUT that's not all, for when I found
   I could not get sweet Nell;
I thought the girl's mother would
   Do almost quite as well,
But what was my amazement when
   I had begun the talk,
To hear her whisper, "Favour me
   With *change for this piece chalk.*"

Jim.

Never say die, never say die, but keep your mind serene Joe
The girls are just as keen to wed as ever they have been Joe
Never say die, never say die, for mother or for daughter,
There's just as good fish in the sea as ever came out of the water.

! I shall turn quite crazy---
　　Insane, stark staring mad;
The mother and the daughter both
　　Have treated me so bad.
So I shall turn teetotal*er*
　　Or drown myself, I'm sure,
For I've been told *cold water* is
　　The only *perfect cure*.

Jim.

Haha ha, haha ha, just keep your mind serene, Joe
The girls are just as keen to wed, as ever they have been Joe
So never say die, never say die, but try some other quarter,
There's still as good fish in the sea, as ever came out of the water.

Yᵉ FABLE OF Yᵉ WOLF AND Yᵉ CHILD.

Air — "The Cavalier."

" 'Twas a beautiful night, and the stars shone bright,
    And the moon on the waters play'd,"
When Tom wouldn't sleep, would yell, scream, and weep,
    Although he'd been drugged by the maid.
For she wanted out, just to go to a rout,
    And a few of her sweethearts to meet,
So she said to the child, "If you don't draw it mild,
    "You'll go to the wolf there for meat."

Now a wolf passing by, overheard the child cry,
    And also the threat of the maid,
So looking for meat, and expecting a treat,
    Sat down at the door and stayed.
Well as "Dalby" was strong, he didn't wait long,
    Till he heard the little boy snore,
So at once he rose up, as he wanted to sup,
    And gently he tapped at the door.

With her heart pit a pat, the maid heard the rap,
    And quickly she cut down the stair,
She thought it was Ned, John, William or Fred,
    Yet slyly she whispered, "Who's there?"
She opened her eyes, gave a scream of surprise
    When she heard the wolf saying, "Come now,
Sure didn't you promise, you'd give me little Thomas
    Because he kicked up such a row."

In a dreadful hurry, in a fright and a flurry,
    She bolted up stairs like a shot,
And slap on his mug, she emptied a jug
    Of water that was scalding hot.
And she said with a jeer, "Don't never come here,
    No, not by no means," says she;
Then he rushed from the door, while loudly he swore—
    "He may yell till he bursts for me."

HAME'S AYE HAME

The bonnie bird that lilts its sang
　Amang the hawthorn trees,
The laverock in the lift sae hie,
　In simmer's morning breeze;
They wadna gie their ain bit nests
　For ony nests they see—
　　For hame's aye hame
　　Wherever it may be.

The fumart and the whitret tae,
　Intil the auld stane wa',
A shelter find frae simmer's heat
　And winter's storm and snaw,
And wadna gie their ain bit lairs
　For ony lairs they see—
　　For hame's aye hame
　　Wherever it may be.

Though folk may gang to ither lands,
    And ither countries praise,
Yet loving hearts aye dwine to see
    Auld Scotland's heathery braes,
And wadna gie their ain auld hames
    For ony hames they see—
        For hame's aye hame
        Wherever it may be.

And though my biggin' is but sma',
    And my bit mailin' wee,
Yet wife and bairnies mak' it aye
    A paradise to me ;
I wadna gie my ain bit neuk
    For ony neuks I see—
        For hame's aye hame
        Wherever it may be.

"LUBLY TOPSY."

Air—"*Lubly Topsy.*"

Oh! tell me truly, lubly Topsy,
   Top, top, top, top, top, top, Topsy,
Will you be my Popsey wopsey,
   Pop, pop, pop, pop, Popsey wopsey.

      Chorus—Den Topsy, darling, come wid me.
                And keep my farm in Tennessee;
                Oh say yes, Topsy, yes oh do,
                For I lub no yaller gal but you.

Dere am two fowl and one ole chicken,
   Chick, chick, chick, chick, chick, chick, chicken,
Dat get dar liblihood by pickin',
   Pick, pick, pick, pick, pick, pick, pickin'.
      Chorus—Den Topsy, darling, come wid me,
         And keep my farm, etc.

Dere am one duck dat does de quackin',
   Quack, quack, quack, quack, quack, quack, quackin'.
Dere wor dhree more, but two am lackin',
   Lack, lack, lack, lack, lack, lack, lackin'.
      Chorus—Den Topsy, darling, come wid me,
         And keep my farm, etc.

And dere am one ole turkey gobbler,
   Gob, gob, gob, gob, gob, gob, gobbler,
Him got one leg, so him one hobbler,
   Hob, hob, hob, hob, bob, hob, hobbler.
      Chorus—Den Topsy, darling, come wid me,
         And keep my farm, etc.

Dere am one dog dat does de barkin',
   Bark, bark, bark, bark, bark, bark, barkin',
Him watch and keep de gals from larkin',
   Lark, lark, lark, lark, lark, lark larkin'.
      Chorus—Den Topsy, darling, come wid me,
         And keep my farm, etc.

And dere am lub and lots of bacon,
  Bac, bac, bac, bac, bac, bac, bacon,
All can be got wid me for de takin',
  Tak, tak, tak, tak, tak, tak, takin'.
Chorus—Den Topsy, darling come wid me
    And keep my farm in Tennessee;
    Oh say yes, Topsy, yes oh do,
    For I lub no yaller gal but you.

Being a continuation of the "Old Whale."

AIR—"*The Whale.*"

Oh all ye lubbers now on land,
    As never was at sea,
And wishes to hear of something nautical,
    Come listen now to me,—Brave boys.

'Twas in the year of onety one,
    On April ye first day,
When with a screw, our galliant crew,
    To the seas did bore away.—Brave boys.

A dead calm wind blew in our teeth,
    Another blew a-lee,
When away our galliant ship she flew,
    And her taffrail ploughed the sea,—Brave boys.

We bored away at the Greenland seas,
  Till we saw a mighty whale,
The tremendous length of which, 'tis said,
  Did reach from the head to the tail,–Brave boys.

The captain on the bowsprit stood,
  With the mainmast in his hand,
"Overhaul, overhaul, let your maindeck fall,
  And belay her to the land, –Brave boys."

We then cut up that whale in two,
  From the nose unto the snout,
And there discivered a grey-haired man,
  As was "all up the spout"—Brave boys.

Our captain was a brave little man,
  And a brave little man was he,
Yet never a word at all he spake,
  But said, "Now who are ye,–Brave boys."

The grey-haired man he turned his quid,
  Says he, " I tell to you,"
" I's the cabin boy as is was lost,"
  " In the year of eighty-two,—Brave boys."

" And seeing as how as I'm on shore,"
  " Leastwise among sich fellows,"
" I'll never by no means go no more "
  " To live in Whaleses bellows—Brave boys."

MORAL.

" So all ye men take my advice,"
  " If a Jonah you would be,"
" Just try it first upon dry land,"
  " Before the sea you see,—Brave boys."

Tilly Fell.

No sound is heard, no evening breeze
    Stirs now the drooping leaf,
For silent Nature seems to blend
    Its sorrow with our grief,
And mourns with us the loss we feel,
    The loss no words can tell,
For oft we miss the fairy form
    Of gentle Tilly Fell.
        Then come and twine the pretty flowers,
            The flowers she loved so well,
        In garlands round the little grave
            Of gentle Tilly Fell.

The little birds that warbled forth
    Their loving notes in song,
And welcomed her with tiny words
    As light she tripped along,
Are silent now, and listless sit
    In Tilly's favourite dell;
For they, too, miss the lovely form
    Of gentle Tilly Fell.
        Then come and twine the pretty flowers,
            The flowers she loved so well,
        In garlands round the little grave
            Of gentle Tilly Fell.

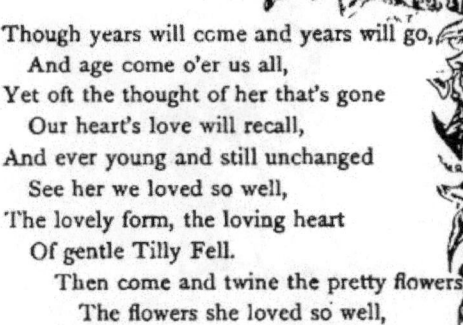

Though years will come and years will go,
    And age come o'er us all,
Yet oft the thought of her that's gone
    Our heart's love will recall,
And ever young and still unchanged
    See her we loved so well,
The lovely form, the loving heart
    Of gentle Tilly Fell.
        Then come and twine the pretty flowers,
            The flowers she loved so well,
        In garlands round the little grave
            Of gentle Tilly Fell.

A GOLDEN RULE IN GOLF.

Air "*The days we went a Gipseying.*"

Oh I love the game of golf, my boys,
   Though there are folks in town,
Who, when upon the Links they walk,
   Delight to run it down.
But then those folks, who don't like golf,
   Of course can't comprehend
The fond love that exists between
   A golfer and his friend.

For on the green, the new command,
   That " Ye love one another,"
Is, as a rule, kept better by
   A golfer than a brother.
For if he's struck, a brother's rage
   Is not so soon appeased,
But the harder that *I hit* my friend,
   The better he is pleased.

Now every rule is said to have
    Exceptions of some kind,
So there is one to this one too
    I always bear in mind.
'Tis in a foursome on the green,
    In play some afternoon,
My friend is wroth, when *on the head*
    I hit him *with a spoon*.

But what is that—a bagatelle
    In this sad world of strife.
As seldom for another will
    A friend lay down his life,
And yet with us oft in a match,
    A golfer keen, 'tis said,
Loves one *who putts him in a hole*,
    Or else *who lays him dead*.

And now, though at this social board
    I may have bored you all,
I trust that no one will decline
    Responding to my call,
Which is to fill your glasses up,
    And drain a bumper full
To golf,—the only game I know
    Which keeps this Golden Rule,
              Chorus—Rule Britannia.

THE SNOWFLAKE

'TIS once, only once that the snowflake falls,
   With its fairy step to rest on the earth,
Till the balmy breath of the south recalls,
   It once again to a heavenly birth.
Returning as gems, in the sparkling showers
   Of the Spring, to gladden the earth anew,
Or as Flora's pearl, on the Summer flowers,
   In the matchless form of a drop of dew.

Though once, only once, if a kind word falls,
   From the lips when the heart is full of love—
It lifts in the cot and in lordly halls,—
   The fainting soul to a heaven above.
And cheering the hopeless by hopes untold,
   Gives life to the lifeless again to live,
Aye, better by far than the selfish gold,
   That charity cold can only give.

If once, only once the kind heart feels,
   The slightest breath of another's woe,
It waits not until the storm reveals,
   The hidden depths of its grief below.
But watching at once for the gentlest breeze,
   And spreading its sails of hope around—
It rests not, until the angry seas
   Of life are calmed and, a haven found.

"BONNIE BAIRNIE."

AIR—"*Bonnie Scotland I adore thee.*"

Bonnie bairnie, how I love it,
None can rob its daddy of it;
Many a one my bairn might covet,
      Bonnie, bonnie bairnie.

Wi' its wee bit nosey-posey,
Cheeky-peekies red and rosy,
And its bosey, cosey-osey,
      Bonnie, bonnie bairnie.
Wi' its bonnie brow brow brenty,
And its mouthie-pouthy dainty,
Made for kissie-wisses plenty,
      Bonnie, bonnie bairnie.
   Chorus—Bonnie bairnie how I love it, etc.

Wi' its e'enie-peenies glancin',
And its leggie-peggies dancin',
Like a horsie-porsey prancin',
    Bonnie, bonnie bairnie.
Kittlie-wittly my bit pussie,
Creepie-crappy up the housie,
Cuddlie-wuddly my ain mousie,
    Bonnie, bonnie bairnie.
  Chorus—Bonnie bairnie how I love it, etc.

Ridie-pidey pownie-owney,
Fallie-pally down, down, downy,
Mendie-pendy, crackie-crownie,
    Bonnie, bonnie bairnie.
Toesie-poesy, feetie-peety,
Handie-pandy, goodie-sweety,
Nicie-picey, eatie-peaty,
    Bonnie, bonnie bairnie.
  Chorus—Bonnie bairnie how I love it, etc.

Cockie-locky henie-pency,
Duckie-pucky, kitty wrenie,
"Cow-wow-wow- ie;"—.nowie thenie.
    Bonnie, bonnie bairnie.
Bedie-pedy, cosie creep in,
Hushy-bushy bairnie sleepin',
Guardian angels watches keepin',
    Ower my bonnie bairnie.

"SCOTLAND'S BONNIE BROOM."

AH! mony, mony fairy sichts
   In ither climes I've seen,
And mony a bonnie flower I've pu'd,
   Wi' a' its rich perfume;
But naething yet has cheered my heart,
   In a' the lands I've been,
Like the bonnie draps o' yellow gowd,
   On Scotland's bonnie broom;
      On Scotland's bonnie broom,
      Auld Scotland's yellow broom,
Like the bonnie draps o' yellow gowd,
   On Scotland's yellow broom.

I MIND fu' weel in days gane bye,
   When callants wild we ran,
And pu'd the bonnie gowans,
   And the scented hawthorn's bloom;
How aft was hushed our merry laugh,
   To list the lintie's sang,
'Mang the bonnie draps o' yellow gowd,
   On Scotland's bonnie broom;
      On Scotland's bonnie broom,
      Auld Scotland's yellow broom,
'Mang the bonnie draps o' yellow gowd,
   On Scotland's bonnie broom.

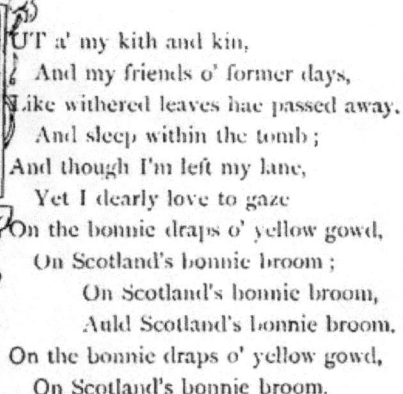

BUT a' my kith and kin,
   And my friends o' former days,
Like withered leaves hae passed away,
   And sleep within the tomb;
And though I'm left my lane,
   Yet I dearly love to gaze
On the bonnie draps o' yellow gowd,
   On Scotland's bonnie broom;
      On Scotland's bonnie broom,
      Auld Scotland's bonnie broom.
On the bonnie draps o' yellow gowd,
   On Scotland's bonnie broom.

THE BREWING O' THE "TUM."

AIR—"*Come Lasses and Lads.*"

Come listen my boys, of all the joys
   That mankind ever knew,
I do declare, 'tis the secret rare,
   Good toddy how to brew.
To waste time 'tis a sin, so let us now begin.
   And we'll make it, make it, make it, make it,
      Make it properly.
Chorus—With a fal de ral al, fal al de ral al, etc.

Be certain you've got the water hot,
   To make your tumbler warm,
Then put in it, of sugar one bit,
   (But two can do no harm).
Then pour the water in, just half way to the brim,
   And stir it, stir it, stir it, stir it,
      Stir it carefully.
Chorus—With a fal de ral al, fal al de ral al, etc.

The whisky then take, and quickly make
   Your tumbler three parts up,
And then you'll find, if to your mind,
   'Tis fit for a king to sup.
But perfection I always seek, so of course recommend an eke,
   And to mix it, mix it, mix it, mix it,
      Mix it thoroughly.
Chorus—With a fal de ral al, fal al de ral al, etc.

The bottle then send across to your friend,
    For him to do the same,
To free this life from care and strife,
    Oh, that is our little game.
So whenever this tumbler's done, we'll just brew another one,
    And drink it, drink it, drink it, drink it,
        Drink it joyfully.
Chorus—With a fal de ral al, fal al de ral al, etc.

But time does pass, so fill your glass,
    For a bumper now I'll give,
To the ladies dear, so drink all here,
    And wish them long to live.
To them let us honour pay, from me take the time of day,
    With a hip, hip hip, hip, hippity hip,
        Hip hip, hip hip, hurrah.
Chorus—With a hip hip, etc.

THE RUIN OF THE "TUM."

Air—"*Cheer Boys Cheer.*"

Drink, boys, drink, and drown here all your sorrow,
Drink, boys, drink, and think not of to-morrow;
What though it be a poison slow you take;
Drink, boys, drink, if but for company's sake.
    What though your money is hardly won and made,
    What though your bills should never once be paid;
    Have you not a right to spend it as you choose?
    Then drink, boys, drink, and never once refuse.

Chorus—Drink, boys, drink, and drown here, etc.
    What though for food your wife and children cry,
    And one after one they dwine away and die;
    Or should they live in poverty and grief,
    Still *you* by drinking can always get relief.

Chorus—Drink, boys, drink, and drown here, etc.
    What though it brings disease, and woe, and crime,
    Surely there's pleasure in drinking at the time;
    What though grim death should find you unprepared,
    Still there's in drinking, a pleasure to be shared.
Chorus—Then drink, boys, drink, and drown here all, etc.

YE FOX AND YE GRAPES,—ANE FABLE.

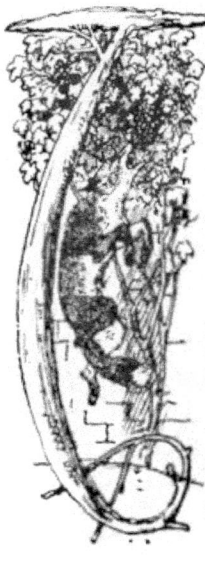
was in the time of Sophocles,
A mighty master of eccles-
Iastic fame kept broccolis
    In his garden.
Carrots and turnips, beans and pease,
A little celery for his cheese,
And many other things like these,
    Not worth a " fardin'."

But then he had some splendid grapes,
Which grew in most fantastic shapes.
Figures of women, men, and apes,
    Yet tasted good;
Black and white, and green and blue,
Scarlet and red, of every hue,
'Twas thus those grapes in clusters grew.
    And grow they would.

People from every quarter came,—
The deaf, the dumb, the blind, the lame,
And always found those grapes the same,
    And so would swear
That better grapes they ne'er could own,
That better grapes they'd never known,
That better grapes they'd never grown,
    Than what grew there.

A fox one day came walking by,
And casting a look towards the sky,
He saw the grapes, cried out " My eye,
    "The chips for me."
He looked around with great delight,
And saw that no one was in sight,
And calculated that he might
    Have two or three.

So in imagination sweet
He almost had begun to eat,
He smacked his lips and rubbed his feet,
    Anticipating
At least that he would take a part,
So he ran back to get a start,
Grew so excited that his heart
    Was palpitating.

After a bit he grew more quiet,
And as he wished to have a shy at
Those splendid grapes, so he leapt high at
    A single bunch.
He missed them by an inch or two,
And then quite fierce and furious grew,
He couldn't get them, and he knew
    He'd lost his lunch.

He tried, and tried, and tried again,
He tried, and tried, with might and main.
He tried, and tried, 'twas all in vain,
    Then gave it up.
So he sat down, said, " By the power,
I've wasted nearly half an hour
To get those grapes ; I think they're sour,
    I'll go and sup ;

" But no, as I'm a red-tailed sinner
I'll see if wife has got the dinner
Ready ; if not, why then I'll skin her,
    And make her roar ;
" And I'll be savage if those boys
Are playing there with all their toys ;
I cannot bear their horrid noise,
    It's such a bore ;

" And now I think those grapes the same
As yon fat, fair, and forty dame
Had on her (you know she's lame)
    When she fainted.
" Yes, yes, she had them on her bonnet ;
Those are the grapes she had upon it ;
And now, " I'll take my davy " on it,
    They are painted."

So, finding that he thus was balked,
He turned about and off he walked,
And muttered to himself and talked
   Of what he'd seen.
When he got home his angry mate
Scolded him for being late;
"The dinner is as cold as slate,
   Where have you been?"

"Been! I, I, I've been," said Mr Fox.
"Why, I've been to see the cocks,
And hens, and chicks;—O, please don't box
   My ears that way."
He took a seat and sat him down
With never a word but many a frown,
Though all the boys throughout the town
   Were there that day.

   MORAL.

If ere a good thing is in view,
Just take it, if you can, to you;
But if you can't, 'twill never do
   To run *it* down.
And if at home you are not kind,
And bear your griefs with cheerful mind,
Though rather late, perhaps you'll find
   They'll run *you* down.

THE MUSIC O' THE CURLING TEE.

Air—"*Behind yon hills.*"

LOE the music o' the burn
   That glints like siller in the sun,
And jinkin' 'neath its mossy banks
   Loups lichtly oot in sport and fun;
And ever warblin' limpid strains,
   Rins rowin' onward to the sea,
But yet there's music sweeter far,
   That winter ever brings to me.

LOE the music o' the word
   That's whisper'd laigh 'mang leafy wuds,
At gloamin' ere the kythin' moon
   Wi' siller tips the fleecy cluds;
Or when the wee bit starnies bricht
   Are glimm'rin' in the lift sae hie,
But yet there's music sweeter far,
   That winter ever brings to me.

OR though nae wimplin' burnie rins
   Wi' lauchin' mirth down to the sea,
Nor whisper'd word o' maiden fair
   Is heard aroun' the leafless tree;
Yet crumpin' snaw aneth the feet,
   And flichterin' flakes afore the e'e,
Tell me the sweetest music is,
   "The music o' the curlin' tee!"

DO ANGELS BID THEM COME?

OH! tell me why do little flowers,
    In beauteous colours bloom;
Oh! tell me why are little flowers,
    So rich in sweet perfume.
Why tiny birds with songs of praise,
    And bees with busy hum,
Linger within our garden fair;
    Do angels bid them come?

Oh! tell me why do gentle rains,
    On lovely flowers alight;
Why dewdrops in the morning gleam,
    Like diamonds sparkling bright;
And when the ground is white with snow,
    Why Robin for his crumb,
So trusting at the window waits;
    Do angels bid them come?

Ah! well I know our sister dear,
    With kind and watchful eye,
Looks down on us, who loved her well,
    From heaven beyond the sky,
And sends, as emblems of her love,
    To all she left at home,
Those lovely tokens from above,
    Yes, angels bid them come.

"WEE NANNIE."

AIR— "*Woo'd and Married an' a'.*"

aince was in love, dyve ye ken,
   I'll ne'er be again, no never,
I canna mak' oot how some men
   Are fa'in' in love, aye for ever.
For I've no been richt o' mysel,
   I'm aye in a kind o' a swither,
Noo mind, gin the story I tell,
   Ye manna let on to my mither.

first saw the lass at a fair,
   The glance o' her e'e wasna cannie,
I dinna ken onything mair,
   But folk aye ca'd her "Wee Nannie."
I ne'er saw the like o' her brow,
   Her hair it was bonnie and curly,
But losh, when I think o' her mou',
   I feel kind o' a' tirly-wirly.

I'm no gi'en to gangin' aboot,
    I'm no gi'en muckle to roamin',
But I fand mysel', when I gat oot,
    Aye nearer her door at the gloamin';
Syne I gied a bit tirl at the pin,
    A thing that I ne'er did afore,
But just as I turned for to rin,
    The lassie she opened the door.

Eh michty! I got sic a fricht,
    I fand mysel dozin' and reelin',
My heart keepit duntin' a' nicht,
    My head a' round about reelin';
I dinna ken how I got placed,
    I dinna weel mind ony mair,
Till my arm was round her bit waist,
    And her on my knee on a chair.

I canna jist weel bring to min',
    How aften we kissed ane anither;
But, losh man! I thocht it was fine,—
    Now, mind ye, ye'll no tell my mither.
At last we got on to the crack,
    Says I, "Will ye be my Nannie?"
Says she, "When neist ye come back,"
    "Ye'd best jist speir at my Grannie?"

The words were scarce oot o' her mou',
    When ben her auld grannie came happin',
And I, without muckle ado,
    Oot o' the back door sune was stappin',
Sin' syne I've been feared to gang back,
    At nicht I feel lanely and eerie,
But I'm sure, gin my meat I could tak',
    I'd sune be as sound as a peerie.

I'll ne'er see the lassie again,
    I'll ne'er tak' a look at anither,
I got sic a gliff wi' the taen,
    My certy, I'll ne'er fash a tither,
When I think o't, I'm gey short o' breath,
    And feel a' kind o' thro' ither,—
Noo mind ye, ye said "sure as death"
    Ye wadna let on to my mither.

THE WAYWARD BOY.

Oh mother, do not weep for me,
Your wild, your wayward boy,
Oh mother, do not weep for me
When all seems bright with joy;
For soon this world I leave for one,
Where none feel grief or pain;
So mother, mother, do not weep,
In heaven we'll meet again.

Oh mother dear, forgive me now
For all those pangs of woe,
Thy sorrowing heart I've made to feel,
Thy loving heart to know;
Oh had I worlds I'd give them all,
To live my boyhood o'er;
But mother, mother, do not weep,
In heaven we'll part no more.

Oh mother, kiss me ere I go,
And clasp me to thy heart;
Yes mother, kiss me ere I die,
One fond kiss ere we part.
Oh mother, haste, for angels wait,
To bear me to the sky:
So mother, mother, kiss me now,
One fond kiss ere I die.

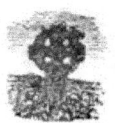

AULD SCOTCH TUNES.
Air—"Green grow the Rashes, oh."

I dinna care for foreign airs,
  Wi' a' their twists and twirlin', O !
They want *the thing* our ain tunes hae,
  That sets the blood a' dirlin', O !
Chorus—For our tunes gang to the heart,
    They're canty and they're cheerie, O !
    We'll sit and sing the lee lang nicht,
    And no be tired, nor weary, O !

Nae doubt, that twa three foreign anes
Are what ye may ca' bonnie, O !
But our auld tunes o' Scottish growth,
Are better far than ony, O !
Chorus—For our tunes gang to the heart,
    They're canty and they're cheerie, O !
    We'll sit and sing the lee lang nicht,
    And no be tired, nor weary, O !

The folk that praise up foreign airs,
"Are nought but senseless asses, O !"
For fient a ane the gree can haud,
Wi' "green grow the rashes, O !"
Chorus—"Green grow the rashes, O !"
    "Green grow the rashes, O !"
    For fient a ane the gree can haud,
    "Wi' green grow the rashes, O !"

O TEMPORA! O MORES!
1863.

AIR—"*Come under my Plaidie.*"

The good times of old are miscalled now-a-days,
   And we take to ourselves all the credit and praise
For fine moral feelings, elevation of tone,
   And a sense of propriety scarce before known;
But in my opinion, 'midst bluster and talk,
   We have need to tak' care o' our steps as we walk,
" For there's ower muckle din for the wee pickle woo',
As the auld deevil said when he clippit the sow."

We sneer at the times, when our fathers cared least
   For the learning they left in the charge o' the priest,
For noo education has reached such a state,
   Each bairnie can read, and can write on a slate,
And each man tak's a paper, wi' leaders so sage,
   And five or six murders and thefts on each page.
" Hech! there's ower muckle din for the wee pickle woo',
   As the auld deevil said when he clippit the sow."

In the good times of old, sir, by hook or by crook,
    Our forefathers rarely could finger a book,
But noo they're sae plenty they quickly get stale,
    Though authors and publishers keep up the sale;
Yet whiles at ilk ither they like a bit dab,
    When ilk ane for himsel' a' the profits would grab.
" Faith, there is ower muckle din for the wee pickle woo',
    As the auld deevil said when he clippit the sow."

We scoff at the times when the churches were rare,
    And the sermons aye lasted some sax hours and mair,
For noo we're sae gude, we can preach them aff hand,
    And sing hymns by proxy, wi' organ and band;
And then wi' bazaars and wi' raffles we try
    To pay off the debt on the steeple sae high.
" Hech! there's ower muckle din for the wee' pickle woo',
    As the auld deevil said when he clippit the sow."

In the good times of old, sir, our forefathers paid
    The tax that the clergy for stipends got made,
But noo we hae men who, for conscience' sake,
    Will no pay what's due on the house that they take;
Till their goods they are seized, and the auctioneer pale,
    With a " towering official," attends at each sale.
" Troth, there's ower muckle din for the wee pickle woo',
    As the auld deevil said when he clippit the sow."

We jeer at the times when our fathers drank yill,
    And took their bit sup wi' hearty gude will,
Mair shame to them too, for they often got fou',
    We only get "drunk and incapable" noo;
But, then, now-a-days little drinking is seen,
    For the law shuts the publics and opes the shebeen.
"Hech! There's ower muckle din for the wee pickle woo',
    As the auld deevil said when he clippit the sow."

In the good times of old, sir, our fathers did dine
    On gude halesome food, and they thocht it was fine.
But noo, gin the Provost or Bailies should gie
    A spread o' a dinner to a Prince or to me,
Then each dish on a card has a Frenchified name,
    Altho' in good Scotch, faith, they taste just the same.
"Ah, there's ower muckle din for the wee pickle woo',
    As the auld deevil said when he clippit the sow."

In the good times of old which are now much abus'd,
    When people cast out then bad language they used,
But noo, for example to set to their herds,
    E'en ministers quarrel and fecht wi' 'Gude Words,"
Which may do the parish the gude that it needs,
    And keep their folk frae illegitimate deeds,—
"But there's ower muckle din for the wee pickle woo',
    As the auld deevil said when he clippit the sow."

The good times of old, ha! we laugh at them, when
    Committees were held irresponsible then,—
When judges cut down the poor advocates' fees,
    And Crawley court-martials crawled slow at their ease;
And when there existed an Act to suppress
    The greatest of humbugs, the Social Congress.
'Troth, they made muckle din, but they baggit some woo',
    Quhilk was mair than the auld deevil did
        When he clippit the sow.

And noo, in conclusion, I've only to say,
    We've nae need to brag about our time o' day,
For, viewed through a glass o' extraordinar'size,
    I canna weel see where the betterness lies.
Sae, in my opinion, 'midst bluster and talk,
    We need to tak' care o' our steps as we walk
"For there's ower muckle din for the wee pickle woo',
    As the auld deevil said when he clippit the sow."

"OH, HEY FOR A CRACK WITH A LASS."

AIR—"*The Campbells are coming.*"

1st part—
Oh, hey for a crack with a lass, with a lass,
Oh, hey for a crack with a lass, with a lass,
I tell you my boys, that the chief of my joys,
Is a cosie bit crack with my lass, with my lass.

2d part—
Let topers sing praise in sonnets and lays,
          To their wine
          So divine,
       As the bottle they pass—
That's nothing my boys, compared with the joys
Of a cosie bit crack with my lass, with my lass.

Chorus— A cosie bit crack with my lass, with my lass,
2d part repeated.
A cosie bit crack with my lass, with my lass,
That's nothing my boys, compared with the joys
Of a cosie bit crack with my lass, with my lass.

Oh, hey for a crack, etc.
    Let rich farmer chields, take pride in their fields.
        In their sheaves,
        And their beeves,
      In their crops and their grass—
That's nothing my boys, compared with the joys
Of a cosie bit crack with my lass, with my lass.
    Chorus—A cosie bit crack with my lass, etc.

Oh, hey for a crack, etc.
    Let soldiers feel proud, and let soldiers talk loud
        Of their wars,
        And their scars,
      With the pride of their class—
That's nothing my boys, compared with the joys
Of a cosie bit crack with my lass, with my lass.
    Chorus—A cosie bit crack with my lass, etc.

Oh, hey for a crack, etc.
    Let rich misers seek, with pale sunken cheek,
        Their pleasure
        In treasure,
      Of dull senseless brass—
That's nothing my boys, compared with the joys
Of a cosie bit crack with my lass, with my lass.
    Chorus—A cosie bit crack with my lass, etc.

Oh, hey for a crack, etc.
    So I'll fill up my glass, and the bottle I'll pass,
        For I think
        I will drink
        In a glass, to my lass—
For I tell you my boys, that the chief of my joys
Is a cosie bit crack, with my lass, with my lass.
    Chorus—A cosie bit crack with my lass.

THE DEWDROP.

HE Sable Midnight rose one day
To woo the Early Morn,
But the coy maiden flew away,
　　Away, away,
　　　On light wings gay,
With laughing glee and scorn;
For Cupid closely watching by
Had quickly let his arrow fly,
　　But missed for once
　　　Ha, ha!

THEN grieving he had missed his mark,
(So much for shooting in the dark,)
His tears fell down in sparkling showers,
And lighting on the early flowers,
　　Lay glistening there,
Till Early Morn and Sunbeam Bright,
　Both laughing at poor Cupid's plight,
　　Did with their smiles the dew drops dry,
　　And thus revived the archer sly.

OLD FRIENDS AND TRIED FRIENDS.

Old Friends and tried friends,
  Old friends and true,
Once more around this board we've met,
  As we were wont to do;
As we were wont to do of old—
  In happy days gone by,
When the sunshine of our friendship true,
  Brought brightness to each eye:
Brought brightness to each eye around,
  While kindly joke and jest,
Were echoed back in merry laugh,
  By friends we loved the best.
So let the joys and happiness
  Of former days, once more
Rejoice our hearts and drive away
  All sorrow from our door.

Chorus—Then pass the wine cup round,
    'Mid mirth and jollity:
  And sing the songs of former days,
    With happiness and glee.
  And we'll swell the chorus loud again,
    'Till rafters ring once more,
  With merry sounds we love to hear,
    As in the days of yore.

Old Friends and tried friends,
  Old friends and true,
Once more around this board we've met,
  Our friendship to renew ;
Our friendship to renew, although
  It ne'er decayed has been,
For memories dear of pleasant times,
  Have kept it ever green.
Have kept it ever green and fresh,
  In full bloom of its strength ;
For early ties of friendship's love,
  Grow closer with their length.
While hearts that once have fondly beat
  Together, tried and true,
Grow warmer as we grasp the hands
  Of friends both old and new.
Chorus—Then pass the wine cup round,
    'Mid mirth and jollity :
    And sing the songs of former days,
      With happiness and glee.
    And we'll swell the chorus loud again,
      Till rafters ring once more,
      With merry sounds we love to hear,
      As in the days of yore.

"THE RETURN HOME OF THE WANDERER."

Mother, mother, dearest mother,
  Take your dying daughter in,
Now a homeless, helpless outcast,
  Borne to earth, by want and sin.
Mother, clasp me in your arms,
  Let me in your bosom lie,
Let me kiss you, dearest mother,
  Once more see your loving eye.

Mother, mother, do not weep now
    Wipe the teardrop from thine eye,
Soon we'll meet no more to sever,
    Meet in realms of bliss on high.
Mother, all the prayers you taught me
    In my heart are deep engraved,
Angels hovering round me whisper,
    Joy in heaven o'er sinners saved.

Ask mankind to spare my "sisters,"
    Tell them that they little know
All their trials and temptations,
    All the griefs of sin and woe;
Ah! 'twere well to treat them kindly,
    Erring sisters though they be;
One soft word in kindness spoken
    Brought back all my love for thee.

Mother, mother, do not curse him,
    Never harshly of him speak;—
As forgiving, so forgiven,—
    Mother, kiss once more my cheek.
Dearest mother, all is dark now,
    Hark, I hear a tolling bell;—
Mother, mother, do not leave me—
    Bless me, mother, fare-thee-well!

THE T, TEETOTALEER.

AIR—*"The Old Irish Gentleman."*

Oh, please don't ask me now to sing,
I'm sure I cannot do it,
I've tried one song for many a year,
But never yet got through it,
For my voice it is *A natural,*
And if I raise one note
I find that it will never do,
The *B* sticks in my throat;
    And I'm sorry that I cannot come
    The operatic style.

One consolation yet I have,
I'll never be at *C* (sea),
I've still a greater, I can get
No nearer to the *D*——;
But this is bad, enough to make
A fellow take the pet,
Whene'er I try to find *G sharp,*
Why then *A flat* I get;
    And I'm sorry that I cannot come
    The operatic style.

But yet, my friends, I must allow
It wasn't always so;
Just listen for a moment while
I tell my tale of woe;
Yes! I could sing! but once, when in
A state of inebriety,
A friend of mine got me to join
A Temperance Society;
   And I'm sorry that I cannot come
   The operatic style.

And ever since that horrid night
When down my name I wrote,
I've a lithp and thta, thta, thtammer on my tongue
And a loud burr-r in my throat,
Tho n-n-now my fr-riendth who w-with to thing,
And k-keep theirr voitheth clearr,
Take m-m-my advith, and n-n-ne'err become
A T-Tee-to-taleerr,
   And th-then, perchanth, y-y-you'll come
   It thtrrong in the o-o-operratic thtyle.

THE GUDE GAUN GAME O' CURLIN'.

AIR—"*Maggie Lauder.*"

Cheer up my lads, for auld John Frost
   His snaw white flag's unfurlin';
And by my troth this year we'll hae
   A gude gaun game o' Curlin'.
For weel ye ken it's John himsel'
   That's at your door pins tirlin',
Sae tak' your brooms, for sune we'll hae
   A gude gaun game o' Curlin'.

When Wintry winds sae cauld and snell
   Blaw doun the lang glen swirlin',
Then Curlers keen begin to think
   Upon the game o' Curlin'.
For weel they ken they meet wi' freens,
   And no wi' auld wives snirlin';
Sae tak' your brooms, for sune we'll hae
   A gude gaun game o' Curlin'.

Aye, though the winds sae cauld and snell,
   A' ither folk are nirlin',
Our speerits rise as ithers fa'
   When e'er we think o' Curlin'.
For naething else can warm our hearts
   Or set our blood a' dirlin';
Sae tak' your brooms, for sune we'll hae
   A gude gaun game o' Curlin'.

Sae cheer my lads, for auld John Frost
    His snaw white flag's unfurlin',
And on the roarin' rink we'll sune
    Our Channel stanes be hurlin'.
But while around this board we sit
    Our cogs and cappies birlin',
We'll drink "Success, and sune to hae
    A gude gaun game o' Curlin'!"

"DINAH VHOE."

AH! Dinah Vhoe, the time at last
    Has come, when my poor heart
No longer beats with earnest hopes
    That we might never part;
For bells are ringing merrily,
    And every one is glad
To welcome now thy bridal hour;
    My heart alone is sad.
Chorus—Then fare-thee-well, and though no more
        Thy fairy form I'll see,
      I'll pray that every blessing may
        For ever rest on thee.

FOND love to me once filled thy heart,
    But, oh! how sadly changed
Since first we met in yonder dale,
    And through the wild wood ranged;
When tiny leaves the secret heard
    Of whispered promise dear;
But leaves and vows alike were gone,
    As winter time drew near.
Chorus—Then fare-thee-well, and though no more
        Thy fairy form I'll see
      I'll pray that every blessing may
        For ever rest on thee.

THOUGH far from thee I'll wander now,
    Forsaken and alone;
Yet I can ne'er forget the time
    I loved thee as my own;
For every bird within the glade,
    Each flower upon the plain,
Remind me of those happy days,
    Which ne'er can come again.
    Chorus—Then fare-thee-well, and though no more,
        Thy fairy form I'll see,
      I'll pray that every blessing may
        For ever rest on thee.

MY AIN WEE BAIRN.

AIR—"*Sensation Duet.*"   *Sung as a Solo.*

Oh! I do love my ain wee bairn,
   Wi' mouthy pouthy merry,
Wi' nosey-posey, bosey cosey,
   Cheekie-peekie cherry.
For it's as good as good can be,
   Like nicey-picey sweetie,
But here's a big dog toming now,
   To eat my pussie cheetie.
      Bow, wow, wow, bow, wow, wow,
         Bow, wow, wow, wow, wattie,
      Doggie eaty pussie cheetie,
         Killy 'itty cat-ie.

And was it fightened that dhe dog,
    Would eat my wee bit mousie?
Go 'way bad dog to bedie-ba,
    And seep in its ain housie.
And so dhe doggie bitet 'ou,
    And gived my baby pain-ie.
Oh! hidey from dhe doggie now,
    For doggie back again-ie.
        Bow, wow, wow, bow, wow, wow,
           Bow, wow, wow, wow, wattie,
        Doggie eaty pussie cheetie,
           Killy 'itty cat-ie.

Oh! no dhe doggie ditn't bite,
    It only matit fun-ie,
It wouldn't eaty my wee lamb,
    Nor hurty any one-ie.
It very fond of 'itty bairns,
    Of 'itty bairns like this-ie,
So clappy doggie on de head,
    And give it sweetie kiss-ie.
        Bow, wow, wow, bow, wow, wow,
           What d'ye think o' that-ie,
        Wasn't that a nicey song
           To sing to pussie cat-ie.

GOLFING SONG.

Air—"*The Lass that loves the Sailor.*"

WHEN swift thro' the air the ball I see flying,
   My heart is rejoiced at the sight,
As away from the tee, whether skimming or skying,
   It speeds like an arrow in flight.
      For 'tis pleasant to know,
        As the ball on doth go,
    That straight to the hole it is spinning;
        But the stroke I love,
        All else above,
        Is the long putt sly
        That steals in by,
    And makes me sure of winning.

AND when thro' the green, 'gainst friend or foe striving,
　With either a long club or short,
'Tis delightful to see the "Grass Beast" you are driving
　Is one of the good running sort.
　　　For 'tis pleasant to know,
　　　As the ball on doth go,
　　That straight to the hole it is spinning;
　　　But the stroke I love,
　　　All else above,
　　　Is the long putt sly
　　　That steals in by,
　　And makes me sure of winning.

AND 'tis pretty to see the ball neatly taken
    From out of a bunker or whin;
And a good quarter stroke, is sure to awaken
    Some hopes of our chances to win.
        For 'tis pleasant to know,
        As the ball on doth go,
    That straight to the hole it is spinning;
        But the stroke I love,
        All else above,
        Is the long putt sly
        That steals in by,
    And makes me sure of winning.

THE GRINDERPEST.

AIR—"*the organ Grinder.*"

You've asked me now to sing a song, I'll try to do my best,
  Altho' I've got the new disease, Punch calls the Grinderpest,
And so I claim your *sufferance* now, for the *sufferings* I've endured :
    For I really cannot take more *pains*, until my
      aches are cured.
    Chorus—For oh what a Guy, I'm sure am I,
      With a bolster for a binder ;
    All twisted and tied about my neck,
      For a nasty aching grinder.

I've had this torture for a month, and suffered night and day ;
  By fasting long, my waist, in short, is wasting fast away ;
No good have I got from the cures my kind friends do advise :
    And at those remedies I quake, queer quacks now
      advertise.
    Chorus—For oh what a Guy, I'm sure am I,
      Spoken—(With one flannel petticoat and) a
    Bolster for a binder ;
    All twisted and tied around my neck,
      For a nasty aching grinder.

Of cures, that mustered by the score, the best was mustard hot,
    And salt has riz a penny the pound from the quantities I bought;
No comfort came from camphor, nor from brandy, oil, or salt:
    At last the cures for toothache came too thick, so I'd to halt.
        Chorus—For oh what a Guy, I'm sure am I,
            Spoken—(With 2 blankets, 1 flannel petticoat and) a
            Bolster for a binder;
            All twisted and tied around my neck,
            For a nasty aching grinder.

Last night I on a dentist called, to learn my fate and doom,
    When with a vice most viciously, he pulled me thro' the room;
Three mortal hours he tugged and pulled, when with an awful scrunch,
    The thing came out and in its grip, 12 sound teeth in a bunch.
        Chorus—For oh what a Guy, I'm sure I'm I,
            Spoken—(With 3 sheets, 2 blankets, 1 flannel
                petticoat, and) a
            Bolster for a binder;
            All twisted and tied around my neck,
            For a nasty aching grinder.

Now when I gently swore at him, to show him my contempt,
    "I think," says he, "its not so bad, just for my first attempt;"
So off I went with lots of pain, without my paying at all,
    When the villain hauled my coat tails off, as I rushed from the hall.
        Chorus—For oh what a Guy, I am sure am I,
            Spoken—(With 4 counterpanes, 3 sheets, 2 blankets,
                1 flannel petticoat, and) a
            Bolster for a binder;
            All twisted and tied around my neck,
            For a nasty aching grinder.

And so good bye, for no good by my stay on land I've found;
   I've groaned this grand grind now so long, I'd grind it underground,
So now I'm off to sea, to see if (as my friends are sure),
   I can upon the ocean wide a remedy *secure*.
     Chorus—For oh what a Guy, I'm sure am I,
        Spoken—(With 5 sets of bed curtains, 4 counter-
          panes, 3 sheets, 2 blankets, 1 flannel
          petticoat, being 15 articles in all, and) a
       Bolster for a binder;
       All twisted and tied around my neck,
         For a nasty aching grinder.

ENCORE VERSE.

Altho' *aloud* you call on me, such calls are not *allowed*.
   For singers find now that no gains, *accrue* without a *crowd;*
And as *encores in course* of time, will be but borne as bores,
   I'll sing *one chorus o'er as* we must not get o'er the scores.
     Chorus—For oh what a Guy, I'm sure am I,
Spoken—(With 2 coal scuttles, 3 dozen dessert knives and forks,
        1 mahogany table and chairs to match, 5 sets of bed cur-
        tains, 4 counterpanes, 3 sheets, 2 blankets, 1 flannel
        petticoat, and) a
      Bolster for a binder;
      All twisted and tied around my head,
        For a nasty aching grinder.

THE AULD FAIL DYKE.

The auld fail dyke that's biggit on
    The bare face o' the brae,
Crown green wi' age when ither dykes
    Wi' crottle are grown grey.
In winter's bitter stormy blasts,
    In winter's nippin' cauld,
Aye gie's its lown side to the wee
    Bit lammies o' the fauld.

The wimplin' burn that rowin' rins
    And glints sae bonnilie,
In arny glen, as it gangs by,
    Gie's life tae ilka tree.
The ferny bank, the mossy stane,
    And whiles a buss o' whin,
Drink deep the jaups the burnie gies
    In lipperin' ower the linn.

The silvery saugh, though auld and gell'd,
    Sends oot a flourish green,
And cosie shiel's the cushie doo
    That croodles late at e'en.
The wee bit chirmin' burdies tae,
    A bield fin' in the wuds,
Afore the lift is cussin ower
    Wi' mirk and rain-fraucht cluds.

E'en sae though poortith cauld be yours,
    Frae nature tak' the lead,
And gie to freens and fremit-folk
    A helpin' hand in need.
For a' your lear and learnin' ne'er
    Can teach ye how to ken
How far intil the waefu' heart
    A kindly word gangs ben.

A HIGHLAND MOTHER'S LAMENT.

DEATH OF RODERICK M'KENZIE, 1745.

STORY—"*See Stewart's Sketches of the Highlanders.*"

CHAN a righ! a mother's heart
    Needs not the cumha's wail,
To tell her only loved one lies,
    In Æonach's wild vale.
The fleetest foot on mountain side,
    The strongest arm in fight,
The bravest heart "MacCoinich" boasts,
    Is cold and low this night.
But when thy kinsmen take the field
    To win back "Charlie's" ain,
Thy foes shall tremble at the cry,
    Of "Tullochard" again.
Though now the "crios madadh ruadh" grows,
    No longer green for thee,
For gone art thou, light of my eyes,
    My Roderick, "laogh mo chridhe."

OCHAN a righ! the thistle now
   Hangs low its drooping head,
The heather and the brechan die,
   In memory of the dead.
For braver heart ne'er loved them well,
   Nor truer held them dear,
But silent is the footfall now,
   A mother loved to hear.
Yet Scotland will remember oft,
   In after years with pride,
And tell, how for her rightful King,
   My loved one nobly died.
      Though now the "crios madadh ruadh" grows,
         No longer green for thee,
      For gone art thou, light of my eyes,
         My Roderick, "laogh mo chridhe."

Ane crovve and ane scheepe,
  on ze seam grene pasture fede.
Zeid ze scheepe to ze crovve,
  "I vvish zou'd scratich mine hede."
Zeid ze crovve, "Govy dick!
  quhy quhat doe zou meane?"
"Gif zou saie zat to me agene,
  quhy I'll picke oute zour een."
"Oh," zeies ze scheepe,
  "ze needna crack lyke zat,
Myselfe has lettel doubt ze ken,
  quhat is ane big B flatte."
Zeies ze crovve vnto ze scheepe,
  "oh fy! oh fy! for schame,"
"I vvondere zat to ane gentleman
  zou vvould use sitch a name:"
"To schow mine grit countempt for zou,
  I'll ride vpon zour backe,"
"Although I thinke zat for ane scheepe
  zat zou are rather blacke;"
"Oh," zeies ze scheepe, "gif ze
  get amang mine vvule
Zou'll very sune find oute,
  zou are quhat is called ane fule."

Ze crovve hee zen iumpt vp,
    and hee lit upon ze maine,
But hee very sune fand out,
    zat hee coudna get downe againe;
Zo ane hirid lad hee did comme vp,
    and hee zeid "Alacke! alacke!"
"Quhat art zou deuing zere, zou rogue,
    vpon zat scheepes backe."
"I heerd zour conversaz-i-on,
    and zou set vp ze chat,"
"Zo I'll take zou for mine deiner,
    as zou seim very fat."
Zayes ze crovve unto ze scheepe,
    "oh now I'll zaie mine zaie"
"For I am zure I neuer will
    zee another daie."

    (YE ZAIE.)

"Gif e'er zou're asked to helpe ane freend,
    zen doe it quhile zou can,
And neuer let ane fause pride,
    doe zou any vvrange."

CURLING SONG.

"A GUDE GAME YET."

An auld man sat ayont the fire,
    A' grewsin' wi' the cauld,
For winter hard had now set in,
    Wi' cheerless blast and bauld.
"I'm surely donner'd turn'd," he said,
    "What gar'd me to forget,
There's nought like curlin' warms the blood,
    We'll hae a gude game yet."

The auld man rose and took his broom,
    And toddled down the glen,
Fu' blythly tae, for weel he kent
    He'd meet his friends again.
And aye he mummled to himsel,
    "What gar'd me to forget,
There's nought like curlin' warms the blood,
    We'll hae a gude game yet."

The auld man stappit on the ice,
    He was nae langer auld,
His hand but touched the curlin' stane,
    He felt nae mair the cauld.
And as he raised the broom, he cried,
    "What gar'd me to forget,
There's nought but curlin' warms the blood,
    We'll hae a gude game yet."

The auld man played as aft he'd played,
    In curlin' days of yore ;
And young men said, "They ne'er had seen
    "Sic bonny play afore."
And as he *hirs't the stane*, he cried,
    "What gar'd me to forget,
There's nought like curlin' warms the blood,
    We'll hae a gude game yet."

The auld man's now aneath the mools,
    He dwined jist wi' the snaw,
And sair we miss his weel kent face,
    His kindly heart an a'.
But aye we'll mind how aft he cried,
    "What gar'd me to forget,
There's nought like curlin' warms the blood,
    We'll hae a guid game yet."

"THE HERRING FISHER."

When seabirds home are flying, as daylight softly fails,
The fisher off to his favourite ground, away from the harbour sails;
    Then *shooting his nets*, he slowly drifts
    With the tide, where fish like wildfire glow.
    Oh! his heart is light, and his hopes are bright,
    As he sees the "buoys" are sinking low.

SHOOTING HIS NETS

At morn, when fresh'ning breezes hasten the fisherman home,
When dashing waves and billows rough, are crested white with foam;
    Then whispers of wife and loved ones play
    With the whistling winds in gladsome glee.
    Oh! his heart is light, and his hopes are bright,
    As his boat *rides over the dark blue sea*.

RIDING ON THE SEA

At times, amidst his fancies, *his pleasant dreams of home,*
He finds a shade of sadness, a tinge of fear will come;
    But love he knows is keeping there
    Her watch with keen and trustful eye.
    Oh! his heart is light, and his hopes are bright,
    Though storms loom in the lowering sky.

Then home with a fair wind blowing, with the first bright gleam of day,
The boat, with her treasure laden, speeds onward thro' the spray;
    And the fisherman, safe in his cottage, finds
    A *welcome warm* awaits him there.
    Oh! his heart is light, and his hopes are bright,
    For he knows love lightens every care.

EAST AND WEST.

Air—"*Hame Cam' our Gudeman at Een.*"

East and west the auld wife look'd,
   East and west look'd she,
And there she saw her youngest son
   Come ridin' ower the lea.
"Oh, hooly, hooly, Sandy, lad,
   And whaur hae ye been,
And what gars ye ilka nicht
   Bide oot sae late at e'en?"
     "Late!" quo he;
     "Ay, late!" quo she.

"Weel, mither, troth, gin ye speir.
   I'll e'en tell to ye,
It's jist twa raws o' pearls white
   That ne'er cam' frae the sea."
     "Pearls!" quo she;
     "Ay, pearls!" quo he.
"Oh, lang hae I lived, lad,
   And mony a place I've been,
But pearls binna frae the sea,
   In troth I haena seen."

East and west the auld wife look'd,
   East and west look'd she,
And there she saw her youngest son
   Come ridin' ower the lea.
"Oh, hooly, hooly, Sandy, lad,
   And whar hae ye been,
And what gars ye ilka nicht
   Bide oot sae late at e'en?"
     "Late!" quo he;
     "Ay, late!" quo she.
"Weel, mither, troth, gin ye speir,
   I'll e'en tell to ye,
It's roses red and cherries ripe
   That ne'er grew on the tree."
     "Cherries!" quo she;
     "Ay, cherries!" quo he.
"Oh, lang hae I lived, lad,
   And mony a place I've been,
But cherries binna frae the tree,
   In troth I haena seen."

East and west the auld wife look'd,
　　East and west look'd she,
And there she saw her youngest son
　　Come ridin' ower the lea.
"Oh, hooly, hooly, Sandy, lad,
　　Ye're unco late this e'en,
Sae noo jist tell me, aince for a',
　　Whar hae ye *been?*"
　　　　"Been!" quo he;
　　　　"Ay, been!" quo she.
("Ay, but that's another question athegither!" quo he.)
"Weel, mither, troth, gin ye speir,
　　I'll e'en tell to ye,
I've *been*, and brought young Jessie hame,
　　My wee bit wife to be."
　　　　"Wife!" quo she;
　　　　"Ay," wife! quo he.
"Oh, lang hae I lived, lad,
　　And mony a place I've been,
But sic a bonny, weel-faured lass,
　　In troth, I haena seen,
And noo I see the rosy blush,
　　The bonny pearly store,
But, Sandy, lad, the cherries ripe,
　　I doubt ye've pree'd afore!"

THE LAST FAREWELL.

AH! well I know the pang it costs,
  To say the word adieu!
Ah! well I know the grief you feel,
  To bid me go from you.
For love alone can know love's woes,
  While words can never tell
The sorrow of the saddened heart,
  That bids you now farewell.
          A long, a last farewell.

BUT in this weary path of life,
  Now lone and dark and drear,
One little star of brightness may
  My drooping heart still cheer.
'Tis when the thoughts of all your love
  Within my bosom swell,
And bring me back to days gone by,
  Farewell, dear love, farewell.
          A long, a last farewell.

AH! those were happy, happy times,
  Too happy long to last;
For all the brightness of their joys
  Like withered leaves are past.
Yet on the pleasures of those days
  My heart will fondly dwell,
Although 'tis sad and joyless now,
  In bidding you farewell.
          A long, a last farewell.

JOHNNY GRAHAM.

Air—"*My Daddie is a Cankered Carl.*"

The fisher a' the summer day, wi' wily art does try,
  To tempt the trout frae out the burn, wi' worm or gaudy fly,
But he may fish the lee lang day, and what d'ye think, care I,
  Oh! its all the same to Johnny Graham,—I've other fish to fry.
      I've other fish to fry, aye, aye,
        I've other fish to fry,
      Oh! its all the same to Johnny Graham,
        I've other fish to fry.

The sportsman toils thro' muirs and woods and fields baith wet and dry,
  In search o' pheasants, hare or grouse, his braw new gun to try,
But he may bleeze the lee lang day, and what d'ye think, care I,
  Oh! its all the same to Johnny Graham,—I've other game to fly.
      I've other game to fly, aye, aye,
        I've other game to fly,
      Oh! its all the same to Johnny Graham,
        I've other game to fly.

The gambler wi' his cheating cards, his cunning trade does ply,
   And tries the green ones to decoy, as a spider does a fly,
But he may play the lee lang day, and what dy'e think, care I.
   Oh! its all the same to Johnny Graham,—I've another card to try.
        I've another card to try, aye, aye,
          Another card to try,
        Oh! its all the same to Johnny Graham,
          I've another card to try.

For there is my own Mary Jane, with smile so sweet and sly,
   Oh! she's the fish, the game, the card, that I mean now to try,
I think o' her the lee lang day, and a' the night forbye,
   And as sure's my name is Johnny Graham, to make her mine I'll try
        To make her mine I'll try, aye, aye,
          To make her mine I'll try,
          For as sure's my name is Johnny Graham
          Fond love beams in her eye.

Rocking herself on her chair,
  With her hands clasped over her knee,
A childless mother, with vacant eye,
  Sees her little children three.
    Her little children three,
    As happy they used to be,
      In the days, long, long gone by.

In the days, long, long gone by,
  For forty years and more
Have passed away, since she heard last
  Their footsteps on the floor.
    Their footsteps on the floor,
    Pattering now no more,
      As in days, long, long gone past.

Rocking herself on her chair,
    With her hands clasped over her heart,
The childless mother, with love lit eye,
    Dreams she has again to part.
        Dreams she has again to part,
        And the same chill's over her heart,
        As in days, long, long gone by.

As in days, long, long gone by,
    And she feels that stifling air
She felt when her youngest and last
    Lay in its cradle there.
        Lay in its cradle there,
        While she watched in the same old chair.
        In the days, long, long gone past.

In the days gone by and past,
    Till rising up slow from her chair
She brings from her only treasured store,
    Three golden locks of hair.
        Three locks of golden hair,
        Hair from three angels fair,
        Fair as in days of yore.

THE YACHTSMAN.

AIR—"*The days we went a Gipsying.*"

Oh, I love the sailor's life, my boys, so boundless and so free,
For like a wild duck on the wing, we plough the dark blue sea ;
And when across the raging deep the stormy zephyrs blow,
We "hoist the capstan on the deck," and "launch the starboard bow."
    We "hoist the capstan on the deck," and "launch the starboard bow."

Oh, I love the sailor's life, my boys, for when it blows a breeze,
We "haul the taffrail hard a port," and "slack the main cross-trees ;"
And when the "swelling shrouds" are filled, we scud across the sea,
And leave the "breakers" far behind, the "scuppers on our lee."
    And leave the "breakers" far behind, the "scuppers on our lee."

Yes, I love the sailor's life, my boys, for when it blows a gale,
We "splice the main-sheet" to the "jib," and then "the rudder brail;"
And if a foeman dare to tread, before our gallant mast,
We "nail the bo'swain" to the "gaff," and cry, "hold hard, avast."
  We "nail the bo'swain" to the "gaff," and cry, hold hard, avast.

The harbour's reached, in safety now, we're anchored to the pier,
So let all hands be piped aloft, the "binnacles" to steer;
And then we'll toast each bounding craft, that skips upon the sea,
For I love the sailor's life, my boys, so jovial and so free.
  For I love the sailor's life, my boys, so jovial and so free.

Yᴱ HARE AND Yᴱ TORTOISE—ANE FABLE.

A Tortoise one day for an airing went out,
  And jolly well pleased looked his face,
As he whistled a snatch of a merry old song,
  Jogging on, at his usual pace.
Now this Tortoise was fat, and had grown very rich,
  And he always wore gaiters and shoes;
Yet respected he was, if people might judge,
  By the nods and "how d'ye do's."

Well, it happened that day, that young Mr Hare,
  Who was reckoned a bit of a spark;
With two or three rabbits, young cousins of his,
  Went out on the spree for a lark.
And as the old Tortoise came trudging along,
  They thought he'd make capital game,
So young Hare, with a wink, cried out, "my old boy,
  "Just pull up and tell us your name."

" Please don't, as you look in such very great haste,"
   Shouted all the young rabbits in chorus;
" But we'll bet ten to one, or whatever you'll take,
   " You won't reach the village before us."
As he wished to get quit of such bothering coves,
   And didn't care much for the tin,
He accepted the bet with each one of them there,
   And took ten to one he would win.

So away they went off, kicked their heels in the air,
   Such laughing, such joking, such fun,
When they thought that the Tortoise was so very green,
   And had been so easily done.
But they hadn't gone far, when they came to an inn,
   Says one, " What's the need of such haste,
" The old boy is slow, and I feel very dry,
   " Who'll come in with me, just to taste."

So each one went in, and called for a pipe,
   And a pint of their best bitter ale,
And they sat and they sang, and they smoked and they laughed.
   And each told a wonderful tale.
They completely forgot they were running a race,
   But at last they remembered the bet,
Each jumped to his feet, and sprang to the door,
   As perchance he might win even yet.

But it proved though the ale they'd been drinking was weak,
    They'd been coming it pretty strong,
For each felt when they measured their length on the road,
    They'd reckoned the distance all wrong.
And they found, as the Tortoise walked over the course,
    That of course the wager he'd won,
So they thought as they shelled out the money to him,
    They had paid pretty salt for their fun.

OH HOW I'VE LONGED FOR THEE.

AIR—"*The Lone Vale.*"

Oh how I've thought of thee, longed for thee, dearest,
Pined to be near thee, beside thee once more;
Oh how I've wearied, thine eye to see, dearest,
Beaming with joy as in bright days of yore,
When by the mountain rills,
When o'er the heathery hills
Roaming, we wandered, while no one was nigh,
When in the wildwood oft
(Dream of my childhood oft)
Love told a tale, in thy dark glancing eye.

Oh how I've longed for thee, waiting and weary,
Yearned from the depths of my sad breaking heart,
Oh how I've pined for thee, life has been dreary,
Sad, sad and lonely since e'er we did part.
Oh to be near thee now,
Kindly to cheer thee now,
Lest aught of danger to thee should come nigh,
Happy defending thee,
Guarding and tending thee,
Loving I'd live for thee, loving I'd die.

"THE STANDARD OF BRITAIN."

High in the heavens our standard is flying,
   Upraised by the arms of the free and the brave;
Ever triumphant, the wide world defying,
   The standard of Britain, still proudly shall wave.
Gay in prosperity's breeze it has fluttered,
   Unmoved it has weathered adversity's blast,
For deep is the oath each Briton has uttered,
    "The flag of our country, we've nailed to the mast."

Bravely our fathers have won us our station,
   A station the foremost in glories renowned,
Raising on high o'er each country and nation
   The standard of Britain where e'er it is found.
There they have kept it, and there it has fluttered,
   Despite of our foemen, for centuries past;
For deep is the oath each Briton has uttered,
    "The flag of our country, we've nailed to the mast."

Keep then as heroes, from heroes descended,
  The greatest of treasures yet left in this world,
And swear, by the homes our fathers defended,
  The standard of Britain shall never be furled.
High let it wave then, and long let it flutter,
  Untarnished, unstained, as in ages gone past ;
For deep is the oath each Briton shall utter,
  "The flag of our country, we'll nail to the mast."

NELLY LEIGH.

Air—"*Nelly Leigh.*"

THE sun shines warm on ev'ry one,
But shines no more for me,
For the brightest day is dark as night,
Without my Nelly Leigh.
She was my only light and love,
The day star of my heart,
And dark, dark is the world to me,
Since ever we did part.
Chorus—Oh, the sun shines warm on ev'ry one,
But shines no more for me,
For the brightest day is dark as night,
Without my Nelly Leigh.

MY Nelly loved the tender flowers,
And prettier was than they,
They knew that, for they bent their heads,
When e'er she pass'd that way.
But now where Nelly lies asleep,
The flowers beside her wave,
And night and day their watch they keep
O'er Nelly's lonely grave.
Chorus—Oh, the sun shines warm on ev'ry one,
But shines no more for me,
For the brightest day is dark as night,
Without my Nelly Leigh.

THE moon is now upon the wane,
The stars begin to fade,
And cast a farewell o'er the dell,
Where my dear Nelly's laid.
But e'er the morning light has shone,
With her again I'll be,
And never, never more shall part
From my own Nelly Leigh.
Chorus—Oh, the sun shines warm on ev'ry one,
        But shines no more for me,
        For the brightest day is dark as night,
        Without my Nelly Leigh.

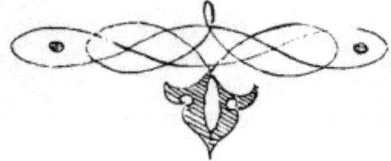

I CANNA LEAVE MY MITHER YET.

Air—*"I'm o'er young to marry yet."*

Oh Lizzie, lass, I've loed ye lang,
   And constant I hae been to thee,
Sae tell me, lassie, will ye gang
   Amang the heathery hills o' Dee.
     I canna gang, I winna gang,
       I manna leave my mither yet,
     For nane can loe her like mysel,
       My ain kindhearted mither yet.

I'll hap ye in my Hieland plaid,
   And keep the wintry cauld frae thee,
Nae ill can harm thee, dearest maid,
   Amang the heathery hills o' Dee.
      I canna gang, I winna gang, etc.

Ye'll wander o'er the ferny knowes,
   And herd the wee bit lambs wi' me,
And pu' the blae that hidden grows
   Amang the heathery hills o' Dee.
      I canna gang, I winna gang, etc.

Noo, Lizzie, dry your fa'in' tears,
   Your mither kind will gang wi' thee,
We baith will tend her fadin' years,
   Amang the heathery hills o' Dee.
      Gin I maun gang, I e'en maun gang,
         An' we shall live thegither yet,
      For nane can loe her like mysel',
         My auld kindhearted mither yet.

DE HAN'SOME NIGGERS.

Air—"De Han'some Niggers."

Dis am de han'some nigger,
And 'sidered quite de swell,
De gals dey all in lub wid him,
Him knows dat bery well.
Chorus—*Yes*, it am Sam,
No, it am Joe,
No, it am Jim,
No, it am Cæsar,
Dat am de han'some nigger.
Dat am de han'some nigger,
Dat am de han'some nigger.
And 'sidered quite de swell.

Dis am de han'some nigger,
Hab wool so bery fine,
Dat from de wing ob de ole crow
Him take out all de shine.
Chorus—No, it am Sam.
Yes, it am Joe,
No, it am Jim,
No, it am Cæsar,
Dat am de han'some nigger,
Dat am de han'some nigger,
Dat am de han'some nigger,
And 'sidered quite de swell.

Dis am de han'some nigger,
   Hab bery tender heart,
Dat neber, till new lub him got,
   Can wid the ole one part.
    Chorus—No, it am Sam,
    No, it am Joe,
    Yes, it am Jim,
    No, it am Cæsar,
    Dat am de han'some nigger,
   Dat am de han'some nigger,
    Dat am de han'some nigger,
    And 'sidered quite de swell.

Dis am de han'some nigger,
   Him true bred in de stock,
And hab a voice so bery sweet,
   Like de female turkey cock.
    Chorus—No, it am Sam,
    No, it am Joe,
    No, it am Jim,
    Yes, it am Cæsar,
    Dat am de han'some nigger,
    Dat am de han'some nigger,
    Dat am de han'some nigger.
    And 'sidered quite de swell.
Grand Chorus—We all de han'some niggers, etc.

MY FIRST MATCH.

Air—"*The Laird o' Cockpen.*"

The morn it is bricht, the sky it is clear,
The frost's sure to haud, the thaw is na' here,
Come awa wi' your brooms, your crampits and stanes,
"Haud fair and foot sure," else tak' care o' your banes.

Now lads, I maun tell you, just dae as you're bid,
  Sae Tam, as you're first, come gie's a *pat lid*,
Na! na! dinna soop, for div ye no see,
  He's ower muckle pouther, he's far past the *tee*.

Now Tam, ye maun look at the way your shot's gane,
  And be sure no to throw awa your next stane,
Gude guid us! he's played just the same as afore,
  He's awa past the tee to the *bank* wi' a *roar*.

Now "Laird," here's the ene- my's stane on the *tee*,
  I'd like you to count wher- ever ye be,
Be sure no to play as Tam's played afore,
  Soop him up! soop him up! he's no ower the *score*.

Next, afore I could gie the "Laird" an advice,
  He threw up his stane, wi' its side on the ice;
'Tak' care o' your legs, let us see where he'll lie,
  Od, Laird! man that's gude, you're nearly *tee high*.

Now Jock, *ye* can play, sae we've naething to fear,
  I'd like ye to lay me just down a guard here.
Hoot's! as plain 's I could speak, I tell't ye to guard,
  But losh, man! ye've broken the back o' the "Laird."

Now tak' ye tent man, when ye next play again,
I'd like ye to tak' the inwick o' this stane;
Faith, "man ye are like," but the *bias* I doubt,
Leads ye aff, sae ye've taen no the *in* but the *out*.

My turn cam' the next, I determined to win,
We cared na for muckle, we just wanted ane,
My stane struck my *cute* (altho' I was skip),
I fell on the ice, and dislocket my hip.

I was awfu' dumfounder'd, and man I was sick,
The doctor attended me mony a week,
I aft wished the stanes and the broom to the deil,
And me, gin I tried another *bonspeil*.

JEDDART JOCK

A BORDER BALLAD.

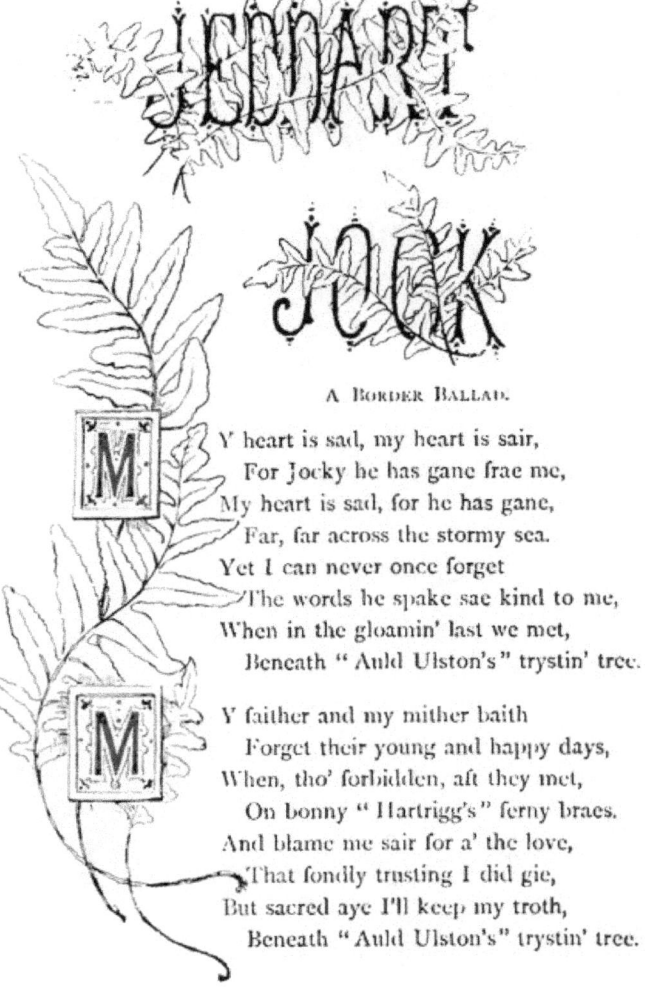

MY heart is sad, my heart is sair,
  For Jocky he has gane frae me,
My heart is sad, for he has gane,
  Far, far across the stormy sea.
Yet I can never once forget
  The words he spake sae kind to me,
When in the gloamin' last we met,
  Beneath "Auld Ulston's" trystin' tree.

MY faither and my mither baith
  Forget their young and happy days,
When, tho' forbidden, aft they met,
  On bonny "Hartrigg's" ferny braes.
And blame me sair for a' the love,
  That fondly trusting I did gie,
But sacred aye I'll keep my troth,
  Beneath "Auld Ulston's" trystin' tree.

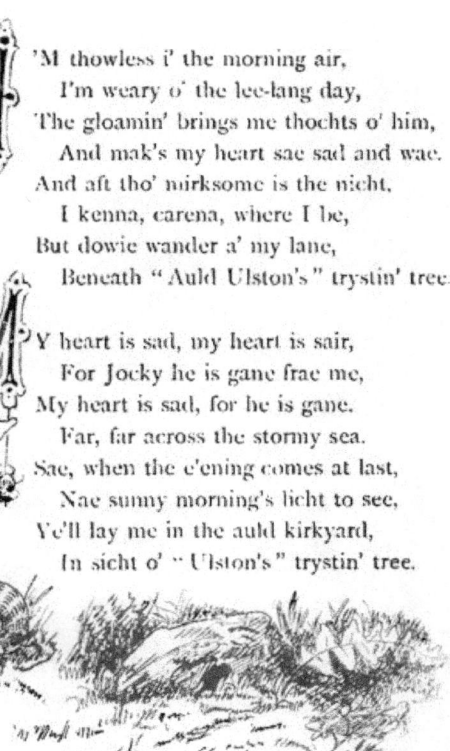

'M thowless i' the morning air,
   I'm weary o' the lee-lang day,
The gloamin' brings me thochts o' him,
   And mak's my heart sae sad and wae.
And aft tho' mirksome is the nicht,
   I kenna, carena, where I be,
But dowie wander a' my lane,
   Beneath "Auld Ulston's" trystin' tree.

Y heart is sad, my heart is sair,
   For Jocky he is gane frae me,
My heart is sad, for he is gane.
   Far, far across the stormy sea.
Sae, when the e'ening comes at last,
   Nae sunny morning's licht to see,
Ye'll lay me in the auld kirkyard,
   In sicht o' "Ulston's" trystin' tree.

WHISKY OH!

AIR—"*Neil Gow's Farewell.*"

Thae folk wha speak in praise o' wine,
Say that it is a drink divine,
But, losh man! its no half as fine
   As gude auld Hielant whisky oh!
  Chorus—Whisky oh! whisky oh!
      Gude auld Hielant whisky oh!
      I dinna think, there is a drink,
      Can match wi' Hielant whisky oh!

And thae wha speak in praise o' beer,
Say it's the thing the soul to cheer,
But, by my troth, it is the mer-
   est trash, compared wi' whisky oh!
  Chorus—Whisky oh! whisky oh!
      Gude auld Hielant whisky oh!
      I dinna think, there is a drink,
      Can match wi' Hielant whisky oh!

Noo, ither drinks are praised by some—
There's brandy, gin, auld Tam, and rum,
But fient a ane's worth the crack o' my thumb,
    Compared wi' Hielant whisky oh !
  Chorus—Whisky oh ! whisky oh !
        Gude auld Hielant whisky oh !
        I dinna think, there is a drink,
        Can match wi' Hielant whisky oh !

For naething, lads, the time can pass,
Like a cosie crack wi' a cheerie lass ;
A weel gaun pipe, forbye a glass
    Or twa o' Hielant whisky oh !
  Chorus—Whisky oh ! whisky oh !
        Gude auld Hielant whisky oh !
        I dinna think, there is a drink,
        Can beat auld Hielant whisky oh !

TA MICMACINTOSHACH.

Air—"*The wee wee Man.*"

Ta great MicMacIntoshach stoot,
Wanst at his cast-ell toor, O,
And there he sawt a sicht he viewt.
He never sawt afore, O.
    He, he, he, ha, ha, ha, ha.

MicMacIntoshach got a fricht,
And nearly rant and flewt, O,
To saw pefore him on that nicht.
Six feet of Cam-ell pluid, O.
    He, he, he, ha, ha, ha, ha.

MicMacIntoshach swore "Gow mach,
Or else your head, I'll proke, O,"
Ta Cam-ell man said, wi' a lauch,
"And did your nainsell spoke, O."
    He, he, he, ha, ha, ha, ha.

MicMacIntoshach cried out, "Drew
You big large Cam-ell dog, O,"
Syne pull-it out his skean dhu,
And givt him a awful prog, O.
    He, he, he, ha, ha, ha, ha.

Ta Cam-ell man he'll fallt down dead.
And then he'll givt a groan, O,
He'll never spokt, and all he'll said,
Was "ach, ech, ich, och hone, O."
    He, he, he, ha, ha, ha, ha.

MicMacIntoshach teuk a sneesh,
And drawt it up his nose, O,
Syne teuk a next, and cried, "Och meish,
So parish all my foes, O."
    He, he, he, ha, ha, ha, ha.

MicMacIntoshach pipers sawt,
Ta carnage from ta first, O,
Wi' joy sae loud ta pipes did blawt,
Themsels and bags was burst, O.
    He, he, he, ha, ha, ha, ha.

Ta great MicMacIntoshach bold,
In rage at large did swore, O,
Syne teuk a drink of water cold,
And fallt dead on the floor, O.
    He, he, he, ha, ha, ha, ha.

MORAL.

MicMacIntoshach's story shews,
A man should stick galore, O,
Ta whisky and ta Athol prose,
And drink water never more, O.

JOCK TAMSON

Air - *John Grumlie.*

John Tamson was a souter gude
   As ever waxed an end ;
And folk frae a' the country side
   Brought him their shoon to mend
For John he was a canty carle
   That worked frae break o' day,
And liked fu' weel to hae a crack,
   Syne bored and chapt away.
      Singing, fal de ral al, etc.

Ae day the curlin' keen began,
  He thocht he'd like to gang :
" Gude wife," quo John, " rax me my broom,
  " I'll no be very lang."
But John he wasna hame till nicht,
  Sae keen was he on play ;
" Gude wife," quo John, " its awfu' fine,
  " I'll gang the morn tae."
    Singing, fal de ral al, etc.

Now John, next morning, kept his word,
  The first time in his life,
And sune forgot his trysted wark,
  His bairnies and his wife.
And aye he played and better played
  Ilk day for mony a week,
And a' the while ne'er chapt a nail,
  Nor yet put in a steek.
    Singing, fal de ral al, etc.

Ae day he rose up early
  And played frae morning licht,
And neither bite nor sup he took
  Till he cam hame at nicht.
Sae John he looket in the pat,
  For a hungry man was he,
" What kind o' kale are thae," quo John,
  " They're unca thin i' the bree."
    Singing, fal de ral al, etc.

"Nae doubt," quo Jean, "the kale are thin,
  "There's neither beef nor banes;
"And ye can sup as best ye can
  "On bree frae Curlin' stanes,
"And ye may learn that while ye play
  "Your bread ye dinna win;
"For tho' there's plenty ga'in out,
  "There's naething coming in."
      Singing, fal de ral al, etc.

John stood amazed, syne loudly swore,
  For an angry man was he;
"Gude wife," quo John, "as sure as death
  "This day you'll dearly dree;"
But better thochts cam' in his head,
  As supperless he lay,
Sae he rose up and took his wark,
  Syne bored and chapt away.
      Singing, fal de ral al, etc.

AIR—"*The Durham Freshman.*"

STEP up and see my museum,
    I've picked every wonder with care,
I'll charge you one penny to see 'em;
    Oh! hang the expense at a fair.

From *Russia* it was the *steps* came, sir;
    The *tiles* from an *old Hatter's stall*;
The *stones* from the *Temple of Fame*, sir,
    The *bricks* from the *Hole i' the wall*.

On the *hinges of Friendship* the *doors*, sir,
    Without any jarring hang well;
And the *locks* from *canals* by the scores, sir,
    Fly back at the sound of *a bell*.

A *cove* fresh from *Cork* just imported,
    As you enter, will take all the tin;
And a *swell* on the *ocean* that's sported
    The *tickets of leave* to get in.

The *quick march of Intellect's* played, sir,
    On the *Trumpets of Fame* as you hear;
And the *singers* in chorus have made, sir,
    A *stave* from a *barrel of beer*.

And now look behind and before, sir,
    Overhead, to the left and the right;
There are things from the roof to the floor, sir,
    But I can't show you many to-night.

Here the *Horns of Dilemma* I've placed, sir,
    With *Pictures of Grief* round the Hall;
And the *Models of Fashion and Grace*, sir,
    In niches are set in the wall.

There is *hair* from the *head* of a fountain,
    From the *head* of a barrel and stick;
There's a *corn* from the *foot* of a mountain,
    'Twould take you a twelvemonth to pick.

There are *teeth* from the *mouth* of a river,
    And also of *Crabb's tales* a part;
But although I haven't the *liver*,
    From a tree there's a bit of the *heart*.

There's the *cloak* that *Hypocrisy's* worn, sir,
    And a *tissue* of *falsehoods* all right;
There's the *fabric of truth* rather torn, sir,
    And an old *sable mantle* of night.

There's the *hands of old Time* and his feet, sir,
    From the *finger of scorn* there's a claw;
There's likewise the *heart of deceit*, sir,
    And a *toe* from a *limb of the law*.

From the *Garden of Beauty* a chair, sir,
    From the *Handbook of Nature* some *leaves*;
An *egg* from the *nest of a mare*, sir,
    And two from the *nest of some thieves*.

There's the tip of the *tongue* of *false Scandal*,
    And also the *eyes of distrust*;
For *screwing up courage* the *handle*,
    And *fetters* that *Love's* often burst.

From an *old laughing stock* there's a *buckle*;
    From the *wheel of misfortune* a *clog*;
Here's a *Colt* that its mother can't suckle;
    And some *bark* taken fresh from a *dog*.

Lying close to the *balance of power*, sir,
    The *scales* too of *Justice* you'll find;
And the *seconds* that lengthen the *hour*, sir,
    Will shew you the *index of mind*.

Now tingle the bell for the waiter,
    For I see it's refreshment you lack,
He'll bring you a *drop of the crater*,
    And a *drop from* "*all's well*" in a *crack*.

If you ask him to bring you a *fork*, sir,
    From a *river* he'll bring it to view;
Don't ask him to pull out that cork, sir,
    For he may take you for a *screw*.

Of a *headland*, he'll bring you the *neck*, sir,
    Or *quarter of globe*, but no more,
As sometimes a nice *little check*, sir,
    Is rather too *large* in the *score*.

He has lots of the *cream of good nature*,
    And some of the *milk* in a can;
And tho' he's been always a *waiter*,
    He's a regular *go ahead* man.

And now if for *rest* you've a notion,
    And nice cosey *blankets* would find,
You can sleep in the *bed* of the *ocean*,
    When you have three *sheets* in the wind.

Now I hope you are pleased with the way, sir,
    I've taken my *steps*, for your *stare;*
And trust that you always will say, sir,
    My *fare* is quite *fair* at a *fair*.

Just tell me you havn't been cheated,
    And are all of you charmed at the sight;
And this Programme will soon be repeated,
    As it seems to have *taken* to-night.

"LIFE."

The moonbeams brightly glancing,
   And sparkling o'er the sea,
On rippling waves are dancing
   And smiling as in glee.
So childhood in the lightness
   Of innocence and joy,
Sees everything in brightness,
   Is charmed with every toy.

And now the clouds are shading
   The bright moon in the sky;
Its beams so softly fading,
   In dark'ning shadows die.
Even so the glow of gladness
   May pass from out the heart,
And hours of pain and sadness
   A gloom to life impart.

But when the dawn appearing,
   Gives light where dusk had been;
The morn with bright ray cheering,
   Enlivens all the scene.
So Love with Hope entwining,
   Will lighten every fear,
And Faith like noonday shining,
   Our Heavenward path will cheer.

"THE JOLLY LOT."

AIR—"*Tramp, tramp,*" *etc.*

Whene'er a jolly lot,
    Together may have got,
And the hours "ayont the twal," they would prolong,
    There's nothing that I know,
    Can make "the pace" to go,
Like a glass or two of toddy, and a song.
  Chorus—So drink, boys, drink, and let's be joyful,
        Sing, boys, sing, and let's be glad,
        For he that drinks should sing,
        So we'll make the rafters ring,
    And we'll echo loud the chorus now like mad.
    2d *Chorus*—Fal lal al de dal de dal dal, etc.

'Tis then that mirth and fun,
    And joke and witty pun,
In their glory always come it fast and strong,
    While the merry tale and jest,
    Ever seem to be the best,
O'er a glass or two of toddy, and a song.
  Chorus—So drink, boys, drink, and let's be joyful, etc.
    2d *Chorus*—Fal lal al de dal, etc.

And we find that friendship dear,
 The Brotherhood sincere
Of hearts that never would each other wrong.
 In closer bonds are knit,
 When for a night we sit,
O'er a glass or two of toddy, and a song.
 Chorus—So drink, boys, drink, and let's be joyful, etc.
  2d *Chorus*—Fal lal al de dal, etc.

So whenever you have met
 With a jovial, jolly set,
And the hours "ayont the twal," you would prolong,
 You will find it is the case,
 You can go a slapping pace,
With a glass or two of toddy, and a song.
 Chorus—So drink, boys, drink, and let's be joyful, etc.
  2d *Chorus*—Fal lal al de dal, etc.

And now before we part,
 I would wish with all my heart,
That you and all who unto us belong,
 May always have a friend,
 Who a jolly night can spend,
O'er a glass or two of toddy, and a song.
 Chorus—So drink, boys, drink, and let's be joyful, etc.
  2d *Chorus*—Fal lal al de dal, etc.

THE GREAT MAY HAE THEIR PALACES.

THE great may hae their palaces,
    Their castles fair and lordly ha's,
But love and peace can dwell as well
    Within the lowly cottage wa's.
Aye mony an ingle-side shines bricht
    When lichted wi's love's lowin' flame;

"IT IS NA AYE Yͤ BIGGEST HOUSE
QUHILK EVER HAS Yͤ MAIST O' HAME"

THE rich may deck themsels fu' braw
    Wi' silks and satins rich and rare;
Yet grandeur often gets a fa'
    And brings to folk baith dool and care.
Aye mony a poor man needna wish
    To change, and tak' a rich man's part.

"IT IS NA AYE Yͤ RICHEST DRESS
QUHILK EVER HIDES Yͤ HAPPIEST HEART"

SAE when contented wi' his lot,
    And kindly love that's a' his ain,
Man's far abune a' warldly pelf,
    And better than wi' warldly gain,
For while his heart is free frae care,
    The ills o' life he doesna fear;

"IT · IS · NA · AYE · YE · RICHEST · MAN
QUHILK · EVER · HAS · YE · MAIST · O' · GEAR."

THE CURLER'S GRIP.

AIR—"*Auld Langsyne.*"

Losh man! I'm glad to see yoursel,
   I'm glad to meet a freen';
But man, the pleasure's greater still
   When he's a curler keen.
      Sae gie's the curler's grip, my freen',
        Sae gie's the curler's grip,
        Losh man! I'm glad to see yoursel,
        Sae gie's the curler's grip.

We've played thegither mony a time,
   Around the curlin' tee,
I've sooped ye aften up the ice,
   You've dune the same to me.
      Sae gie's the curler's grip, my freen',
        Sae gie's the curler's grip,
        Losh man! I'm glad to see yoursel,
        Sae gie's the curler's grip.

Man! when I feel a grip like that,
　I'm unca sweir'd to part;
The blood rins din'lin' up my arm
　An' warms my very heart.
　　　　Sae gie's the curler's grip, my freen',
　　　Sae gie's the curler's grip,
　　　　　Losh man! I'm glad to see yoursel,
　　　　　Sae gie's the curler's grip.

But as the nicht is gye weel thro',
　Let's hae anither "nip,"
An' drink success to ilka ane
　That kens the curler's grip.
　　　　Sae gie's the curler's grip, my freen',
　　　Sae gie's the curler's grip,
　　　　　Losh man! I'm glad to see yoursel,
　　　　　Sae gie's the curler's grip.

OUR HIELANDMEN.

Air—"*A Highland Lad my Love was Born.*"

Whae daurs to say our Hielandmen,
Frae haugh and hill, frae strath and glen,
Are no as brave as when of yore
They fought wi' targe and braid claymore;
Whae daurs to say our Hieland bluid,
Is no as pure, is no as gude,
As when the clans wi' sword and shield,
Were foremost in the battle field.
Chorus—Sing hech, sing how, our Hielandmen,
Our gallant, brave, braw Hielandmen,
We'll mak' them welcome hame again,
Sir Colin and his Hielandmen.

'Twas nae degen'rate bluid I ween
That first on Alma's bank was seen,
When Colin wi' his men in front,
Sae bravely bore the battle's brunt.
Nae braver deed was dune that day,
At Balaclava's bluidy fray,
Than when the Russian horse did feel,
The "thin red line that's tipt wi' steel."
Chorus—Sing hech, sing how, our Hielandmen,
        Our gallant, brave, braw Hielandmen,
        We'll mak' them welcome hame again,
        Sir Colin and his Hielandmen.

And now, 'neath India's burning sun,
Words fail to tell the deeds they've done,
Yet in the charge and daring burst,
The "Hieland bonnets" are the first.
God speed our gallant Hielandmen,
Our gallant, kilted Hielandmen,
Whae highest in the roll o' fame,
Hae raised auld Scotland's honour'd name.
Chorus—Sing hech, sing how, our Hielandmen,
        Our gallant, brave, braw Hielandmen,
        We'll mak' them welcome hame again,
        Three cheers for Colin and his men.

I'M WEARY, WEARY WAITING.

AIR—'*The wearing of the Green.*'

O H! I'm weary, weary waiting,
   Waiting for thee to come home,
Never more from me to wander,
   Never more from me to roam.
Oh, to bring thee back in safety
   To my lonely aching heart,
Never more from thee to sever,
   Never more from thee to part.
    But I'm weary, weary waiting,
      Waiting for thee to come home,
    Never more from me to wander,
      Never more from me to roam.

O H! I'm weary, weary waiting,
   Days have seemed to me as years;
And those years had been a lifetime,
   Had I doubting thoughts or fears.
But my heart is ever hopeful,
   Hopeful trusting for the best,
Watching for thy safe returning,
   Close to clasp thee to my breast.
    But I'm weary, weary waiting,
      Waiting for thee to come home,
    Never more from me to wander,
      Never more from me to roam.

OH! I'm weary, weary waiting,
   Waiting for those happy days,
When thou'lt be for ever near me,
   When thou'lt be with me always.
Then I'll bid thee love's fond welcome,
   Love's fond welcome to my heart,
And we never more shall sever,
   Never, never more shall part.
   But I'm weary, weary waiting,
      Waiting for thee to come home,
   Never more from me to wander,
      Never more from me to roam.

Yᴱ FOX AND Yᴱ CROW.

ANE FABLE.

"ONCE on a time," as old wives say,
    It happened that a crow
For grub had scratched a summer day,
    But found it was no go.

So coming back quite in the huff,
    He passed a cottage door,
And saw a piece of cheese, enough
    To serve some three or four.

He thought if stolen bread was good,
    'Twould be the same with cheese,
So stole it; and as quick's he could
    He flew among the trees.

Now so it chanced, upon that day,
    A fox, a cunning dog,
Lazy and listless, there he lay
    Full length upon a log.

And when he saw the crow alight
    O'er head, upon an oak,
He wished so much to have a bite,
    That cunningly he spoke.

"Why, goodness gracious, mercy me,
    I really, 'pon my word,
Ne'er thought that I should ever see,
    So beautiful a bird!

With plumage glossy black, and clear,
  Just like the raven's wing,
Oh, I should wish so much to hear,
  This beauteous creature sing!"

The crow, delighted with this praise,
  Said, "Really I don't know
A single tune that I could raise,
  I'm hoarse as any crow."

"Well, I'm so sorry," said the fox,
  "It is the case I fear,
But in my pocket I've a box
  Of Locock Wafers here.

They're very good for cough or cold,
  For asthma, hoarseness too,
Excuse me, sir, for being bold,
  But just try one or two."

The crow scarce touched one with his claws,
  Ere he began a song,
The cheese fell to the Fox's jaws,
  But there it wasn't long.

For o'er his throat it quickly went,
  Without e'er saying grace,
Then off he set for home, content-
  ment beaming in his face.

The crow now having twigged his loss,
    Sat on the twig displeased,
Then gave his stupid head a toss,
    And said, " I'm fairly cheesed.

Still I've a comfort I can tell,
    And so my mind's at ease,
I can't have a got a mighty sell,
    When it's just skim milk cheese."

And I will say, the rascal might
    Be punished for the theft,
For to that cheese he had no right
    Unless it had been left.

THE ANGEL SAYS "COME."

SHE sat by the side of her loved one then lying
    On his death-bed dying,
    Still keeping unweary
    Her love watches dreary.
When she *heard* in low whispers his voice softly sighing,
        "The angel says, come."

SHE saw that the smile o'er his thin lips then straying,
    For the last time was playing,
    Yet no useless regretting,
    No chiding, no fretting,
Dimmed the love in her eyes that still bid him be staying,
        For the angel said, "come."

YES, the love in her eyes from her full heart o'erflowing,
    Like watchfire was glowing,
    Yet the mourner, no weeper,
    Watched o'er the death sleeper,
And no dewdrops of grief o'er her wan cheeks were showing,
        When the angel said, "come."

FOR she grudged not the flower, though lone and forsaken,
    The Giver had taken,
    Nor lone watchings dreary,
    Nor dreary nights weary,
As she *felt* that her faith in His love was unshaken,
        Though the angel said, "come."

OUR AULD PUNCH BOWL.

AIR—"*The Bottom o' the Punch Bowl.*"

Come now my boys, and 'midst our joys
   Let's sing in praise o' our Punch Bowl,
And wi' gude will, our glasses fill,
   To drink "gude luck" to our Punch Bowl.

Its no sae famed because it's braw,
   For it's no gowd nor siller gilt,
But it's just for we ken fu' weel,
   There's aye a gude brewst brewed intil't.
      Chorus—Sae come my boys, and 'midst our joys
          Let's sing in praise o' our Punch Bowl,
          And wi' gude will, our glasses fill,
            To drink "gude luck" to our Punch Bowl.

Ilk brewst is brewed wi' meikle care,
    Ilk brewst is brewed wi unco skill,
There's ne'er a headache intilt' a',
    Just come and pree it, gin ye will,
        Chorus—Sae come my boys, etc.

An' when we meet, we fill it fu',
    And toom it tae,—at least we try,
But aye we mak anither eke,
    And never see the bottom dry.
        Chorus—Sae come my boys, etc.

It joins us a' in friendship's bonds,
    An' mak's us brithers ane and a',
It mak's us tae, wi kindly heart,
    To think o' them that's far awa.
        Chorus—Sae come my boys, etc.

We needna care for jealous looks,
    Nor yet for envy's scorn or scowl,
When freen's sincere, frae far and near,
    Fu' canty meet round our Punch Bowl.
    Chorus—Sae come my boys, and 'midst our joys,
        Let's drink "gude luck" to our Punch Bowl,
      To thee and thine, to me and mine,
        And ilk ane round our auld Punch Bowl.

WHEN SUMMER SUNS ARE DYING.

AIR—"*When Summer Suns.*"

When summer suns are dying,
  And fading in the west,
When ev'ning winds are sighing,
  And wooing all to rest;
E'er yet the moonbeams glancing
  Steal lightly o'er the sea,
To kiss the wavelets dancing,
  And smiling in their glee.
When all is still
  O'er heath and hill,
'Tis thus I sing to thee.
Oh, rest thee lady, sleep, love,
While angels hov'ring near
    Their guardian watches keep, love,
      Around thee, lady dear;
    Their guardian watches keep, love,
      Around thee, lady dear.

Yes, when the day is blending,
　　And mingling with the night,
Each fading ray then lending
　　Enchantment with its light.
Ere yet the bright stars shining
　　Dispel the 'witching power
Of ev'ning shades entwining,
　　In twilight's lovely hour.
When all is still
　　O'er heath and hill,
'Tis thus I sing to thee,
Oh, rest thee lady, sleep, love,
While angels hov'ring near,
　　　　Their guardian watches keep, love,
　　　　　　Around thee, lady dear ;
　　　　Their guardian watches keep, love.
　　　　　　Around thee, lady dear.

GOOD NIGHT.

The silent midnight onward creeps, and softly steals away
Each lingering ray the twilight keeps in memory of the day.
So sorrow, ever watching near, will dim love's glowing light,
When heart and soul of friendship dear, must say the word good night.
        Good night, good night.

And happy as we may have been with friends we know sincere,
Yet sadness falls on every scene, as parting time draws near.
And shades the pleasures of the day, that else seemed clear and bright,
For while affection bids us stay, we echo back good night.
        Good night, good night.

Good night.

www.ingramcontent.com/pod-product-compliance
Lightning Source LLC
Chambersburg PA
CBHW031444160426
43195CB00010BB/839